Praise

M000284641

If you want to make a difference through your day job, then this book is for you. *Good Work* is a very practical guide that takes you through each iterative step to convert your passion into purpose and pay. It dispels the myths around finding a new job and leverages Shannon Houde's 20 years of recruitment experience to give you the hiring manager's perspective. Unlock the secrets you never knew about how to position yourself to be relevant to hiring managers and recruiters alike, while growing your knowledge and networks around the issues you care most about. This is a must-read for anyone wanting to make a career change into impact.

JOEL MAKOWER, CO-FOUNDER, CHAIRMAN AND EXECUTIVE EDITOR, GREENBIZ GROUP INC

Shannon Houde's *Good Work* is an invaluable tool for anyone seeking to attain a job that harmonizes personal purpose with the objectives of organizations in the impact economy. A career coach with specialized focus on the impact economy, Shannon has supported many emerging leaders in navigating their paths to meaningful work that aligns who they are with what they do. Now, with her best-in-class book *Good Work*, she has offered a detailed road map – a profoundly valuable how-to process to land a job in the impact sector. If you buy one book to assist you in your work/purpose journey, this is the one!

PETER LUPOFF, CHIEF EXECUTIVE OFFICER, NET IMPACT

Shannon Houde has dedicated her career to catalysing sustainable development through empowering and mobilizing human capital, both as a coach and as a hiring manager. By providing

Good Work

*How to build a career that makes
a difference in the world*

Shannon Houde

KoganPage

Publisher's note

Every possible effort has been made to ensure that the information contained in this book is accurate at the time of going to press, and the publisher and author cannot accept responsibility for any errors or omissions, however caused. No responsibility for loss or damage occasioned to any person acting, or refraining from action, as a result of the material in this publication can be accepted by the editor, the publisher or the author.

First published in Great Britain and the United States in 2021 by Kogan Page Limited

2nd Floor, 45 Gee Street	122 W 27th St, 10th Floor	4737/23 Ansari Road
London	New York, NY 10001	Daryaganj
EC1V 3RS	USA	New Delhi 110002
United Kingdom		India
www.koganpage.com		

Kogan Page books are printed on paper from sustainable forests.

Hardback	978 1 78966 574 1
Paperback	978 1 78966 572 7
eBook	978 1 78966 573 4

British Library Cataloguing-in-Publication Data

A CIP record for this book is available from the British Library.

Library of Congress Cataloging-in-Publication Data

Library of Congress Cataloging-in-Publication Data is available.
Control Number: 2020050242

Typeset by Hong Kong FIVE Workshop, Hong Kong
Print production managed by Jellyfish
Printed and bound by CPI Group (UK) Ltd, Croydon CR0 4YY

CONTENTS

ACKNOWLEDGEMENTS

I have to start by thanking my co-editor, Sara E Murphy. Without her I couldn't have brought together all of my resources, knowledge, anecdotal stories and compelling case studies into this book. Her calmness, meticulous attention to detail, challenge to my thinking, and fun spirit kept me sane through this long process.

I'd like to deeply thank my more than 1,000 coaching clients from over 25 countries who, over the past decade, have trusted me to be their career journey partner in propelling their impact forward. They have opened my eyes to this evolving impact economy, while giving me a deep sense of personal purpose to help others become the change leaders that the world needs.

A special thanks to those who offered to have their personal stories featured in this book: Adrianne Gilbride, Chantal Beaudoin, Christina Forst, Courtney Bickert, Dana Schou, Dave Stangis, Emilie Goodall, Haley Lowry, Hannah Green, Mariana Souza, Mario Elias Gonzalez, Neeraj Agarwal, Peggy Brannigan, Rachel Gordon, Rochelle March, Scott Miller, Tim Mohin and Victoria Moorhouse.

I would like to thank my business manager, Sadie Finch, who is the engine behind Walk of Life and whose tolerance, patience, business savvy and detail orientation has helped to grow the quality of our client relationships over these past few years.

I would also like to thank my amazing parents, Elsa and Glenn, both university academics, for teaching me the value of writing well and sharing knowledge and for being my cheerleaders throughout all of my career achievements.

I also would like to thank Andrew Cartland of Acre recruitment services, who in 2009 encouraged me to create this first-of-its-kind impact careers course and then co-marketed it with me for more than four years. He saw the potential of my vision to support candidates on their journey towards impact jobs that also allowed me to create the lifestyle career I had always wanted.

And last but never least, my young boys, Maximilien, 12, and Austin, 10, who every day thank me for all of the hard work I do for our family. This recognition and encouragement has given me the courage and energy to turn a project like this into reality. I want to leave the legacy of shaping a better planet and communities for them, their generation, and beyond.

Introduction

Making a difference

So, you want to make a difference? Maybe you're feeling uninspired in your job. Perhaps you sense there's something more for you out there in realizing your life's purpose. The number one reason people come to me for support is because they want to feel their careers are making a difference – that they're working toward something bigger than profits and the bottom line. They want to be able to get out of bed in the morning and be excited to go to work, knowing they're having a measurable impact on a higher cause. I love that altruism! Whether you call it purpose, meaning, impact, calling, or self-actualization, the words don't matter as much as the mission: to convert that fire in your belly into results bigger than self, and to get paid to do it.

- Have you ever wondered how you can find a career in which you're making a difference in the world, or if your dream job even exists?
- Do you want to work for an organization that fosters resilience, empathy, diversity and inclusion?

- Have you pondered whether you can really turn your passion into purpose – and pay?
- Are you struggling to land an interview for a purpose-driven job?
- Do you want to know where you fit into the impact sector, or how your skills are transferrable?
- Are you unsure how to tailor your CV or résumé to a job that makes a difference?
- Do you wish you understood how to stand out among the other 150 applicants per job posting?

If any of those questions apply to you, or you wonder what you're doing wrong, then you're not alone – and this book is for you.

A note on semantics

As an American who has lived in Italy, Chile, Switzerland, and currently the United Kingdom, I struggle with linguistic differences every day. (Ask any American who's tried to shop for 'pants' in London!) In this book, I'll be using the words 'CV' and 'résumé' interchangeably.

Similarly, the terminology surrounding what we call 'sustainable business' is constantly changing and being reinvented across time, sectors and organizations. Here are just some of the terms and buzzwords you might see:

- CSR (corporate social responsibility);
- corporate responsibility;
- sustainability;
- inclusive economy;
- ESG (environmental, social, governance);
- EHS (environment, health, and safety);
- resilience;

- purpose-driven;
- human-centred;
- impact investing

…just to name a few! It's hard to keep up, but these terms all essentially convey the same thing: an endeavour to make a positive difference to our environment and communities while driving business, donor or investor returns.

John Elkington, one of the pioneers in sustainable business, created the term 'triple bottom line' back in the 1990s to include returns not only in profits (financial), but also in people (social) and planet (environmental). I really like this concept, as it holds for both individuals and organizations. We all need to earn a living, but we need to do so in a way that is not damaging the human and natural capital on which we rely to generate that financial result.

In this book, we'll use the phrase 'impact for the purpose economy', or the 'impact sector' for short, which encompasses most of the above buzzwords. Sometimes I may interchange words like sustainability or purpose, but these are all referencing the same thing – they reference whatever you define as your impact space.

TIP Use your words

For you to land a job in the impact sector, it's important to know the language of your audience and to match that in your personal branding. Do you want to work in the public or private sector, or for a non-profit or non-governmental organization (NGO)? The language will vary greatly depending upon the space that interests you. For example, what the private sector refers to as 'business development' may be called 'corporate partnerships' or 'fundraising' at an NGO and 'grant giving' in the public sector – but we'll go into this more later in the book.

Just remember: semantics are inconsistent, but underlying ideas are not. It's best to stay open initially, and once you have narrowed down your target in Steps 3 to 5, you can choose the semantics that best match that of your audience.

My 'good work'

It took me 39 years to find my calling. I've spent my career reinventing myself, again and again. I have been a corporate recruiter, a management consultant, an accountant, an entrepreneur three times and a conservationist. I changed jobs every 18 months until I created my own ideal job with Walk of Life Coaching, at the intersection of all the hats I had worn. I realized there was no one-stop resource interwoven with real-time recruitment market intelligence to help candidates who wanted to create or find jobs that aligned with their greater life's purpose, something that took them through the pragmatic and tangible step-by-step journey of making their career change. I saw that my own purpose was to help others convert their passion into purpose and pay. Now I help my clients to land their dream jobs in the impact sector, and thereby to create lives with meaning.

During my more than 20 years working in corporate responsibility and sustainability for and with big brands such as Deloitte, Barclays, Vodafone, Homebase, Adobe and World Wide Fund for Nature (WWF), as well as my time as a corporate recruiter, I observed a gap in the market. There are plenty of recruitment agencies working to help companies find talent, but none of these agencies support the candidates – the jobseekers who want to shift into a career with meaning. The candidates were left to figure it out on their own, which means that many missed out on opportunities they could have landed with a better strategy and step-by-step guidance. I founded Walk of Life Coaching to fill that gap.

Over the years, clients have come to me for help with a diverse set of challenges, blocks, or fears, including the following:

- 'I don't understand enough about where I fit into the sustainability jobs market.'
- 'I want to get better at articulating my skills and telling my career story.'
- 'I'm not sure which impact jobs could fit my skills and background.'
- 'I need to update my CV but I don't know how to make it stand out for the impact sector.'
- 'I want to know how to maximize my LinkedIn profile for the purpose economy.'
- 'I'm confused as to why sustainability recruiters aren't calling me back.'
- 'I hate networking because it seems so "salesy".'

I'm willing to bet that you've had a few of these thoughts yourself – which is where this book comes in!

Who this book is for

This book is a resource for anyone who wants to find a career path or portfolio career that has meaning, is linked to a greater purpose that benefits the environment, communities, and the bottom line, and is aligned with their authentic self. Within that context, there are several different types of jobseekers whose journeys will differ depending on the type of change they're trying to make and their stage in their careers. This includes, but is not limited to:

Sector changers: These jobseekers wish to take the work they're doing now and apply it to a new sector or industry. In this group, I include not just those pursuing a change from, say, retail to the energy sector, but also from non-corporate to corporate or from consulting to in-house, or vice versa.

Role changers: These jobseekers are looking to change their role or function but within their existing sector. They may be aiming for a promotion, to transition to a new job function, or to switch from marketing into cause-related marketing or from finance into sustainable investing.

Newbies and returnees: This category covers jobseekers who don't have much of a recent professional track record or who are trying to break (back) into a career. This includes both recent graduates as well as more seasoned professionals returning to work after an extended absence to raise children, care for a loved one, pursue an advanced degree, or take a long trip around the world (don't we all wish!).

Freelancers and social entrepreneurs: The freelance movement is growing, and a growing number of people want flexibility and autonomy in their work, but individuals don't know how to create what we now call the 'portfolio career' path and make it a viable option for themselves. Meanwhile, entrepreneurial ventures called 'social enterprises' are getting more traction and public funding for their ideas that solve a global or local problem. However, these entrepreneurs need help in formulating their mission, developing their brand and marketing strategies, and competing for funding. The process outlined in this book for a jobseeker is, in essence, the same as for the entrepreneur or freelancer. It is about getting clear who your audience is and then building your brand messaging. In the case of freelancers and entrepreneurs, human capital *is* the product, so you have to get smart about how to present and sell that product.

You may see yourself in more than one of these categories, and that's fine. Later in the book, we'll talk about the importance of changing only one thing at a time, and you'll develop the compelling stories and tools to be relevant and strategic in planning for the transition into your ideal job.

How to use this book

This book is divided into four parts: The market landscape; Aim your compass; Map your story; and Step into the market. Within these parts are 14 steps – each a chapter in this book.

IMPORTANT

It's important to take this journey in chronological order. It's not completely linear, but it is iterative, so please don't skip ahead to the step about CV or cover letter. I know it's tempting, but trust me, there's a reason for the order of the steps!

In Part One: The market landscape, we'll examine the lay of the land and the key players in the impact sector, helping you to unpack the trends at play. In Part Two: Aim your compass, we'll venture into getting you more targeted about identifying the impact job for you, mapping your values and traits, and overcoming the fears or blocks that may be holding you back from taking the leap into a purposeful career change. In Part Three: Map your story, you'll learn how to create your personal story and marketing materials on paper by dissecting impact job descriptions, translating your skills, writing a dynamite CV using accomplishment statements, and overcoming the dread of writing a cover letter that centres purpose. Finally, in Part Four: Step into the market, you will begin to launch your job search in the impact sector with powerful networking tools, including writing a compelling bio, building your personal brand on LinkedIn, being strategic with sustainability recruiters, and learning to pitch yourself like a pro with purpose.

As with anything worth doing in life, building a career with impact for the purpose economy takes effort, and the more you put into the process, the more you will get out of it.

Purpose is personal, change is challenging, and aligning your career with your authentic self requires you to engage at a deeper level than one would normally associate with a job search.

You might find some of this work to be surprisingly emotional, as it can prompt you to ask tough questions of yourself. I invite you to consider what you value most in your life.

What was the 'ah ha!' moment that got you here? Did any of it come easy? I'd bet not. We are all on a continuous journey. This process is no different, but if you're willing to put in the work, you will come out the other side a more fulfilled and impactful change leader.

So now we embark together on this step-by-step journey to convert your passion into purpose and pay, and to build that legacy you envision of leaving the world better than you found it. You've got help now, so anything is possible. Let's make your fantasy career a reality, together.

PART ONE

The market landscape

Lay of the land

What is an impact career?

N ow it's time to get down to business. But first, I want to make sure you've read the Introduction, because it provides important information about how to use this book. If you haven't done so, please go back and read it now. I promise you'll be glad you did!

Great – now that you've read the intro, let's establish what we mean when we talk about impact careers.

Why this step is important

This step lays the groundwork for helping you to understand the sometimes nebulous impact market and the landscape in which we're operating. I'll provide an overview of the impact sector, and we'll look at trends in the purpose economy market and sustainability jobs and hiring. We'll also cover career change tips that relate specifically to this market.

The case for a purpose economy

Surveys have shown that almost two-thirds of workers are either not engaged with, or actively disengaged from, their jobs (Harter, 2019).

Think about that: *nearly two out of three workers* spend *half their waking lives* doing things they don't really want to do in places they don't particularly want to be.

Purpose increasingly underpins both individual and corporate behaviour, and the results are impressive. Research found that those companies that both define themselves by *and* act with a sense of purpose outperformed the financial markets by a whopping 42 per cent (DDI, The Conference Board, and EY, 2018). Additional research found that purpose-driven employees are more loyal and tend to be superior performers compared with those motivated by money and advancement. Further, purpose-driven people have a greater sense of wellbeing throughout their lives and live longer (Imperative and LinkedIn, 2016).

You are a purpose worker. You are special, and because of that, you will have greater meaning in your life and work.

Picture purpose

As we kick off our 14-step journey together, it helps to start by evaluating what exactly impact – or 'making a difference' – looks like for you. Is it about finding your purpose or calling, engaging in meaningful work that helps others, saving the planet, fighting for justice, or simply being your authentic self?

It's easy to get caught up in the present moment and needing a job *today* (or yesterday). That's a real-life challenge and I totally get it. But when it comes to finding your dream impact job, you need to start thinking about what you care about and what you're going to do to put your stake in the ground around certain key issues like renewable energy, human rights, greenhouse gas emissions (GHGs), impact investing, or diversity and inclusion.

SHORT PURPOSE REFLECTION

Take a moment to write down your thoughts on these things before going further:

How will you know in five years that you've made a difference?

_____

_____

_____

_____

What will impact look like for you? Visualize it in detail.

_____

_____

_____

_____

Who will you have affected, where will you have had an impact, and what will have been the purpose?

_____

_____

_____

_____

Purpose drives us all toward our own form of happiness. What do you love doing?

_____

_____

_____

_____

What are you good at?

_____

_____

_____

What issues do you care most about in the world?

_____

_____

_____

_____

There are still further considerations. Do you want a traditional role within a sustainability-focused company or a sustainability-oriented role within a traditional organization? Do you envision changing a big, multinational company from the inside, helping to change the organization from within, or do you prefer a more nimble, start-up environment? We will dive into these decisions in more detail in Steps 3 and 4.

Now let's take an introductory look at the impact sector. This will help you to start developing a sense of how you might fit into it.

Impact sector overview

The impact sector is thriving as global issues become more pressing, evolving quickly in terms of semantics and sub-sectors, and constantly growing. The space itself is not especially well defined. Broadly, the impact sector centres on minimizing environmental and social risks and maximizing environmental and social well-being. Looking at it through a business lens, Erika Karp, founder and CEO of Cornerstone Capital, describes corporate sustainability as 'the relentless pursuit of material progress towards a more regenerative and inclusive economy' (Murphy, 2020).

First, it's critical to start off with the basics. There are a few foundational underpinnings of the impact space with which any serious contender must be familiar. If you want hiring managers, recruiters, or potential clients to take you seriously, you need to be able to talk about these like they are a second language. I recommend that you take some time to research all of them further, if they're not already part of your knowledge base.

Case Study   Victoria Moorehouse

Victoria made the change from a Big Four management consultancy, taking an interim step at the Sustainable Restaurant Association. She is now the Corporate Responsibility Programme Manager at Costa Coffee. For Victoria, understanding the landscape was key to her ability to craft a career transition plan.

Reflecting on the time she spent researching the impact sector, she said, 'Reading the white papers and blogs recommended in this step helped me to demystify the sustainability landscape. I felt like once I understood my target market and their issues better, I could see how an interim step would make my transition more feasible.'

Global frameworks

SUSTAINABLE DEVELOPMENT GOALS (SDGS)

More than 190 world leaders have committed to 17 Sustainable Development Goals (SDGs) to help us all end extreme poverty, fight inequality and injustice, and fix climate change. To successfully build a career in this space, you need to be aware of the SDGs and how companies and governments are implementing and responding to these goals. As a basic first step, look up the SDGs to see all 17 goals and learn more about how they are defined, related targets and indicators, and the progress business and society has made toward each one.

UN FRAMEWORK CONVENTION ON CLIMATE CHANGE (UNFCCC) AND CONFERENCE OF THE PARTIES (COP)

The United Nations (UN) holds an annual climate change conference where the parties to the UN Framework Convention on Climate Change (UNFCCC) come together to propel this agenda forward formally. It's good to stay abreast of the policies and targets that come out of this crucial meeting, known as the Conference of the Parties (COP). I urge you to look up details about past and future meetings, and get acquainted with how each one has moved the climate change agenda along (or not) in its own unique way.

> The pace at which countries have been ratifying the agreement shows that the policy leadership is there to achieve real change. Now we need to work together for a rapid transition to a future built on clean, renewable energy.
>
> Steve Howard, Chief Sustainability Officer, IKEA Group (Rowling, 2016)

Standards and indices

Many of the reports and standards that are used in the impact space are focused on environmental criteria. The 'Big Four' consultancies – KPMG, Ernst & Young (EY), Deloitte, and PricewaterhouseCoopers (PwC) – and boutique assurance providers tend to focus on measuring and reporting issues such as climate change, energy, environment, health and safety, greenhouse gas emissions (GHGs) and carbon offsetting. The tools used to measure and report on these things are established standards, such as:

- The Task Force of Climate-related Financial Disclosures (TCFD): voluntary, consistent climate-related financial risk disclosures for use by companies in providing information to investors, lenders, insurers and other stakeholders;
- CDP (formerly the Carbon Disclosure Project): a global disclosure system for investors, companies, cities, states and regions to manage their environmental impacts;
- The International Standard on Assurance Engagements 3000 (ISAE 3000): an assurance standard for compliance, sustainability and outsourcing audits; and
- The AA1000 AccountAbility Principles (AA1000AP): a framework and guidance for identifying, prioritizing and responding to sustainability challenges.

These standards deal with content that has traditionally been called 'non-financial reporting' because it isn't an audited element of a company's annual report. However, more companies are now reporting this data, indicating an expanding view in business that it drives bottom line results as well. Indeed, many thought leaders in the impact sector argue that this type of information is financially material, especially when it comes to climate change risk management.

More recently, a trend has evolved to include social issues such as human rights, diversity, equity and inclusion (DEI) and wellbeing in corporate and organizational reporting. The Social Progress Index (SPI) provides a rich illustration of how these topics are evaluated. The SPI is produced by the Social Progress

Imperative, which works to make the concept of social progress as important as economic growth or gross domestic product.

The three main pillars of the SPI are basic human needs, foundations of wellbeing, and opportunity. The SPI was designed to measure nations' wellbeing beyond the limited signals provided by purely economic metrics, with the aim to highlight social and environmental considerations in the policy and corporate arenas.

Various standards and indices now incorporate social factors, primary among which are:

- The Global Reporting Initiative (GRI) Standards: a set of global, modular standards for sustainability reporting; and
- The Sustainability Accounting Standards Board (SASB) Standards: a complete set of 77 globally applicable, industry-specific standards that identify the minimal set of financially material sustainability topics and their associated metrics.

I encourage you to look up and familiarize yourself with these standards and indices, as impact practitioners should have a general understanding of them.

Market trends

It's always important to consider the big issues that are trending, including investment trends, as you build a career with impact for the purpose economy. Every year we are faced with challenges across our communities, political landscapes and corporate contexts, and it's important that you stay up to speed on the trends affecting your target audience. You may need to research further:

- **Legislation:** new laws can create risk or opportunity for your target organizations.
- **Global context:** trade, environmental issues, multilateral agreements.
- **Local context:** what is affecting your country, state, city? What are local leaders prioritizing?

- **Environmental shifts:** extreme weather events, changes in natural resource availability.
- **Scientific knowledge:** what is providing more evidence that these issues matter?
- **Workforce trends:** how is the work landscape shifting as new generations and mindsets come into play?

While these issues evolve quickly over time, at the time of writing, here are the major issues shaping the world around us.

CONTROVERSIAL WORLD LEADERS AND A GLOBAL TREND TOWARD NATIONALISM AND PROTECTIONISM

Major economies have been experiencing volatility, uncertainty, complexity and ambiguity (VUCA) stemming from isolationist, nationalist political agendas. This comes at a time when many of the world's greatest challenges – such as climate change, refugee migration and pandemic risk – require multilateral collaboration and solutions.

THE GROWING IMPORTANCE OF SUSTAINABILITY WORK IN THE FACE OF SOCIAL AND ENVIRONMENTAL CHALLENGES

There is a growing recognition that sustainability professionals' work is becoming ever more important, and this isn't limited to non-profits or governments. The private sector is increasingly framing its role in the world beyond simply generating financial profit. Many business leaders now talk about 'stakeholder capitalism', meaning a system under which corporations serve the interests of their shareholders (capitalism), but also serve the interests of their employees, suppliers, communities, and others who are affected by their activities (stakeholders).

In 2020, some of the world's largest investors issued strong statements about the imperative for companies to integrate purpose into their organizational DNA. Larry Fink, CEO of BlackRock – the world's largest asset manager – asked companies in his 2020 annual letter to CEOs to explain what social purpose they serve, and outlined a stronger stance on ESG issues in general and climate risk in particular:

> The importance of serving stakeholders and embracing purpose is becoming increasingly central to the way that companies understand their role in society. **As I have written in past letters, a company cannot achieve long-term profits without embracing purpose and considering the needs of a broad range of stakeholders.** A pharmaceutical company that hikes prices ruthlessly, a mining company that shortchanges safety, a bank that fails to respect its clients – these companies may maximize returns in the short term. But, as we have seen again and again, these actions that damage society will catch up with a company and destroy shareholder value. By contrast, a strong sense of purpose and a commitment to stakeholders helps a company connect more deeply to its customers and adjust to the changing demands of society. **Ultimately, purpose is the engine of long-term profitability.**

We are seeing more proof in the financial markets that sustainability drives financial results. Institutional investors expect to see continued growth in sustainable investment around the world and private equity firms are increasingly making forays into responsible investment and environmental, social, and governance (ESG) performance evaluation and management. That said, there remains a wide gap in this space between concern and action: private equity firms are recognizing sustainability challenges but generally haven't yet done much to address them. That is beginning to change in 2020, as some of the world's largest private equity firms announce major initiatives to integrate ESG considerations into their strategies, and to invest more heavily in sustainable businesses.

Sustainability budgets have been shifting, too, and growing overall. Lately, companies have been investing more in addressing social and environmental issues in their supply chains, developing products and services with a responsible business focus, and engaging with employees on issues that matter to them.

RENEWABLE ENERGY

The energy sector faces upheaval as it seeks to meet two goals that sit somewhat in tension with each other: to reduce human-induced greenhouse gas emissions that are fuelling climate change, and to expand energy access to the millions of people who lack it. As part of this, renewable energy uptake has expanded considerably and reached (and in some cases surpassed) cost parity with conventional fossil fuels, and the transportation sector has begun to electrify.

INCREASING SUPPORT FOR THE UN'S SUSTAINABLE DEVELOPMENT GOALS AS A PROGRESS ROADMAP

While the SDGs were developed for United Nations member countries, business leaders are increasingly adopting them as a framework for their own corporate purpose, and investors with an environmental and social lens are increasingly using the SDGs to benchmark the sustainability of their investments.

WORKERS' PREFERENCE TO WORK AT PURPOSE-LED AND MISSION-ALIGNED ORGANIZATIONS

Across sectors and regions, younger workers increasingly express and demonstrate a desire for work with meaning, and to contribute to organizations that confer a benefit on the world around them and/or help to solve the many social and environmental problems around us. Meanwhile, there has been a growing, organized employee backlash movement at some of the world's biggest companies, including Google and Amazon, against corporate activities that have a negative environmental or social impact.

These global issues trickle down to the marketplace, driving trends in the business landscape. In the 20 years I've been in this space, we've seen growing sustainability teams and job opportunities, and sustainability increasingly embedded into core business. The sector looks very different from how it did when I got my MBA in 2004! Reputation and opportunities for market growth are the major drivers of action, and the UN SDGs are increasingly shaping strategy. At the same time, CSR and sustainability roles in many companies remain limited, and workers generally don't see sustainability as a priority for corporate leaders. Resource use and emissions continue to outpace business efficiency gains, and prioritization of sustainability issues is still more driven by risk management than by value-creation.

> Jobs targeting the inclusive economy could surge as colliding factors of increasing awareness, divided nations, and a rising acknowledgment of needing to do their part as businesses come together. We'll need facilitators, researchers, writers, academia, communicators, project managers, programme managers, fundraising experts, campaigners, policymakers, lobbyists, scientists, social media experts, and a whole host of other skills to fill these.
>
> Ellen Weinreb, recruiter (Weinreb, 2016)

Sustainability jobs and hiring trends

Sustainability teams are growing within corporations and job opportunities along with them. Increasingly, employees from cross-functional departments within an organization will help to deliver sustainability, showing that it is more embedded across core functions. No longer a stand-alone issue or a nice-to-have, we are seeing that more senior-level sustainability roles are joining the C-suite.

Salaries, budgets and headcount in sustainability roles have all been increasing in recent years. At the same time, three out of four millennials would take a pay cut to work for a more sustainable company, according to research by Swytch. Nearly 40 per cent of millennials have chosen one job over another because of how they viewed the company's sustainability, and more than 40 per cent of millennials have committed more time and effort to a company because they were happy with its sustainability agenda (Sproull, 2019). Essentially, a new generation coming up through the workforce increasingly sees being a responsible business as mandatory.

THE IMPORTANCE OF NETWORKING

Networking is as important as ever, especially in more senior roles, which are obtained through human connections rather than job boards more than two-thirds of the time. In fact, most jobs are filled through networking and almost three-quarters are never even posted online (GreenBiz, 2018). If you're not networking, you're missing out! We'll talk about that more in Step 13.

Something to be aware of is the growing focus on intrapreneurship. An intrapreneur is entrepreneurial *within their own organization*, being innovative, taking initiative and proactively creating new programmes. It means helping to embed impact initiatives into core business. Another key trend is that specialists are thriving over generalists, so it's time to drill down and make choices, rather than casting your net wide. In Step 7, we'll look at how to find your niche, rather than relying on your generalist skillset.

Money matters

Despite being impact-focused, each of us also cares about salary. We need to make a living, after all. Over the past decade, salaries in the impact sector have risen modestly, with salaries for some job categories almost flat. When it comes to a trade-off between your salary and your sanity, a career with impact for a purpose economy – even at a pay cut – may well be the right overall choice for you. For many, the fulfilment that comes from the knowledge that you're serving a larger purpose is a trade-off well worth making.

As someone who has been through this process, I was surprised at how having less money made me better off in the long term. When I started my career coaching business, I transitioned from a cushy corporate consulting job at a Big Four consultant in the city to a start-up impact career as my own employer in the countryside. Yes, this change came with a huge pay cut. However, I also became my own boss and gained unmatchable flexibility (for daily meditation, yoga and school runs) and a growing sense of making a difference that I personally couldn't achieve in a big organization.

Even if a pay cut is necessary, though, nobody's suggesting taking a step back in level or role. In fact, making a lateral move is recommended, rather than a lower-level role: it's rare that a hiring manager will want to hire or manage someone who is overqualified. Plus, by taking too much of a step down, you risk devaluing your personal brand.

If a pay cut is likely for you, doing a bit of research will give you a lot of insight into what you can expect. Acre publishes its CRS Salary Survey every other year, and it's a great resource to give you a snapshot of trends in the impact sector in terms of salary, function, sector and more.

Timing

Jobseekers always, understandably, want to know how long it will take to find a job. The more senior you get, the fewer roles are available in the market.

> **TIP** How long does it take?
>
> I have found in working with more than 800 candidates over the years that, on average, it takes one month of job searching for every $10,000 you want to earn.

This means you may need to start a lot earlier than you thought you would! I usually say between six to nine months is a good average, with the starting point being when you have done all the prep work in this book and are ready to start networking and applying to open roles.

Career change tips

You might well be looking to change your job or career, as opposed to making a brand new start. If this is you, here are a few tips to smooth the way:

1 Change one thing at a time. If you try to change too many things at once, the market won't know what to do with you. We will be unpacking this more in Step 3 when we look at the different elements that you should change, one at a time.
2 Consider an interim step. You may need to ease into a bigger transition with a shorter-term transition plan. We'll look at this more in Step 5.
3 Don't apply below your level. If you do, hiring managers won't respect you, you won't get calls for interviews, and you can find yourself in a downward spiral as you wonder why you can't even land junior roles. We'll cover this aspect further in Step 6.

Key resources

White papers

It's easy to get overwhelmed with the amount of white papers, blogs and articles that find their way into our inboxes every day. Here is my curated list of some that I would encourage you to read to get a general sense of the sustainability jobs market. Note that if you're focusing on a few key areas or issues that are less related to corporate sustainability, you will need to seek out sources that are more specific to your focus areas and sector. (We will work more on focusing in Step 3.)

- BSR's annual 'State of Sustainable Business Report' – https://www.bsr.org/en/topics/reports/Sustainability-Management (archived at https://perma.cc/6VKE-UDEX)
- GreenBiz's annual 'State of the Profession' report and 'State of Green Business Report' – https://www.greenbiz.com/reports (archived at https://perma.cc/72D3-4VXB)
- Acre, Carnstone and Flag's annual 'The CR & Sustainability Salary Survey' – https://crsalarysurvey.com/home (archived at https://perma.cc/7Y75-7A4R)
- Net Impact's 'Corporate Careers that Make a Difference' – https://www.netimpact.org/sites/default/files/documents/corporate-careers-make-difference.pdf (archived at https://perma.cc/93ZT-TY7M)
- SustainAbility Trends (updated annually) – https://trends.sustainability.com/ (archived at https://perma.cc/F2UQ-CPG7)
- Circle Economy's annual 'Circularity Gap Report' – https://www.circularity-gap.world/ (archived at https://perma.cc/KS3F-SXL4)

Blogs, news, and organizations

Here are my favourite industry blogs, news outlets, and organizations that I follow. It's by no means an exhaustive list, but it's a strong place to start. It's always good to look at people you admire on LinkedIn to see who they're following, as well:

- GreenBiz – https://www.greenbiz.com/ (archived at https://perma.cc/EGB6-PUZ4)
- Sustainable Brands – https://sustainablebrands.com/ (archived at https://perma.cc/DGJ7-LCH8)
- 3BL Media – https://www.3blmedia.com/ (archived at https://perma.cc/97VK-PJV2)

- Triple Pundit – https://www.triplepundit.com/ (archived at https://perma.cc/L8DK-RH6E)
- CSRwire – https://www.csrwire.com/ (archived at https://perma.cc/J8HP-HVU9)
- Ethical Corporation – https://www.ethicalcorp.com/ (archived at https://perma.cc/J7WE-VYMS)
- Talent Show – https://www.greenbiz.com/blogs/featured/talent-show (archived at https://perma.cc/YFV8-A85V)
- Walk of Life Coaching – https://walkoflifecoaching.com/insights/ (archived at https://perma.cc/EVJ7-4WG7)

KEY POINTS

In this chapter, we looked at the importance of:

- being able to speak fluently about the foundational elements of the impact sector, and staying up to date;
- giving yourself enough lead time in the job search process;
- getting comfortable with the potential reality of trading off big money for big purpose.

What's next?

In the next chapter, we will be launching into Step 2, where we will learn more about the players – who's who in the sustainability and impact sector – as well as potential career tracks.

References and further reading

Note: Many of these are updated annually, so search for the titles to find the latest.

BSR (2018) [accessed 27 September 2019] *The State of Sustainable Business 2018* [Online] https://www.bsr.org/reports/BSR_Globescan_

State_of_Sustainable_Business_2018.pdf (archived at https://perma.cc/77YT-3SNC)

DDI, The Conference Board, and EY (2018) [accessed 27 February 2020] *Global Leadership Forecast 2018: 25 Research Insights to Fuel Your People Strategy* [Online] https://www.ddiworld.com/glf2018 (archived at https://perma.cc/KR23-ZJC6)

Fink, L (2020) [accessed 27 February 2020] *A Fundamental Reshaping of Finance* [Online] https://www.blackrock.com/corporate/investor-relations/larry-fink-ceo-letter (archived at https://perma.cc/XG77-CX94)

GreenBiz Group (2018) [accessed 27 September 2019] *State of the Profession 2018* [Online] https://www.greenbiz.com/report/state-profession-2018-report (archived at https://perma.cc/AK7Q-7ZPW)

GreenBiz Group (2019) [accessed 27 September 2019] *2019 State of Green Business* [Online] https://www.greenbiz.com/report/2019-state-green-business-report (archived at https://perma.cc/N2MX-UZE7)

Harter, J (2019) [accessed 27 February 2020] 4 factors driving record-high employee engagement in U.S., *Gallup*, 4 February [Online] https://www.gallup.com/workplace/284180/factors-driving-record-high-employee-engagement.aspx (archived at https://perma.cc/NH9M-A4EH)

Imperative and LinkedIn (2016) [accessed 31 October 2019] *Purpose at Work: The largest global study on the role of purpose in the workforce* [Online] https://cdn.imperative.com/media/public/Global_Purpose_Index_2016.pdf (archived at https://perma.cc/Y6AB-FXC3)

Murphy, S (2020) [accessed 26 February 2020] On the money: 8 takeaways from the 2020 GreenFin Summit, *GreenBiz*, 10 February [Online] https://www.greenbiz.com/article/money-8-takeaways-2020-greenfin-summit (archived at https://perma.cc/ZY6Y-VDKF)

Rowling, M (2016) [accessed 25 October 2019] Clock starts ticking to implement Paris climate deal, *Reuters*, 6 October [Online] https://www.reuters.com/article/us-climatechange-paris-views/clock-starts-ticking-to-implement-paris-climate-deal-idUSKCN12612D (archived at https://perma.cc/R463-JDEP)

Sproull, D (2019) [accessed 22 October 2019] New study shows employees seek and stay loyal to greener companies, *Medium*, 14 February [Online] https://medium.com/swytch/new-study-shows-employees-seek-and-stay-loyal-to-greener-companies-f485889f9a7f (archived at https://perma.cc/29PT-7JQR)

Sustainability Leads (2017) [accessed 27 September 2019] *2017 State of Sustainability Careers Report* [Online] http://sustainabilityleads.com/jobsreport/r63jl85sxjgww9fk4stkt8u9ouvutf (archived at https://perma.cc/Y5XK-BVEA)

Weinreb, E (2016) [accessed 28 October 2019] How sustainability professionals must lead in 2017, *GreenBiz*, 15 December [Online] https://www.greenbiz.com/article/how-sustainability-professionals-must-lead-2017 (archived at https://perma.cc/2L3E-8M8T)

The change makers

Who do I want to be when I grow up?

Now that we've got the lay of the purpose economy land, let's talk more about the players. In Step 2, we'll focus on identifying the key people in the impact market, in order to build a networking map. This map will in turn help to launch what we'll call a 'soft job search' – ready for more focused targeting in Step 3 and active networking in Step 13.

Why this step is important

People are often keen to skip this step, and just get stuck right in to action. It's understandable; I think we all want it to be easy. We just want to be able to hop online, find a job that looks interesting, apply to it, get the interview, and get the job! But the market simply doesn't work that way for the vast majority of people, and there's a reason the steps go in the order that they do. The behind-the-scenes research of Step 2 is necessary to guide your personal branding and positioning. You need to know who else is doing what you want to do – how else will you know how you stack up as a candidate? Or even what jobs are out there? This is the important research into what is happening in your market areas of interest, so that you gather crucial information for your job-search strategy.

TIP   Using LinkedIn to plan before action

LinkedIn is a key tool for this step. However, we'll look at this platform in much more detail in Step 10, especially where building a personal public profile is concerned. Don't reach out to anyone just yet – for now, you're mapping who the players are and unpacking what ignites your passion at a more specific level, rather than just wanting a job that 'makes a difference'.

The market and the agenda are constantly changing, as is the language surrounding them. Reporting lines aren't always clear or consistent. There isn't always a direct route to your dream job, and you might need to take an interim step. This all means that you are going to need resilience in this process – both as a practitioner once you get the job, and now as the jobseeker. Spending time now to gather all of the information that you will need can only help you, and skipping this step might well hinder you in your efforts to land the right job for you.

Case Study   Dana Schou

Dana made use of her private sector and non-profit leadership expertise, and engaged with her strong network, to positively shape her own sustainability agenda. In so doing, she reached her goal of becoming a philanthropy lead for UNICEF. In reflecting on her work to understand the players in the impact sector, Dana said:

I always knew I wanted an impact-driven job, but I didn't know what jobs were out there. Doing a soft job search – profiling similar people in this space – really helped me understand the types of positions and their keywords, so that I could better match myself to the right roles.

Embrace the ambiguity

The sustainability space is nothing if not ambiguous. Back in 1964, Supreme Court Justice Potter Steward said, 'I know it when I see it' (FindLaw Attorney Writers, 2016). He was talking about the challenges associated with definitions and setting precedent in law, but his comment also applies to the 'hard to define but easy to recognize' paradox of sustainability careers. The industry can be notoriously elusive when it comes to pinning down a technical definition: the lexicon itself is riddled with unhelpful buzzwords that mean different things to different people, the talent pool is heterogeneous, and nobody's *quite* sure what sustainability practitioners actually do.

However, that uncertainty can be a major advantage for those entering the field, because it means that there isn't just one role or one route to a sustainability job: there are many. What's more, building on your strengths can help you carve out your own pathway. Sustainability jobs can and should exist anywhere within an organization; they can be broad and overarching or specific and niche and, increasingly, companies are getting on board with the idea that leaders should be supported, no matter where they sit in the organizational structure. Armed with the research and plans you're going to gather, embrace the ambiguity and figure out how to make it work for you.

Maximize your appeal

This is where it becomes really important for you to explore what impact looks like for you. We introduced this concept in Step 1, and now it's time to flesh it out. What do *you* care about, and which key impact issues mean enough to *you* to put your stake in the ground? When it comes to sustainable change, there is no blueprint to follow – what works for someone else won't necessarily work for you. It's important to play to *your* strengths and passions – knowing clearly what these are will allow you to understand more clearly what those key players want, and to maximize your appeal as a candidate.

Apart from defining what impact means to you, you can maximize your appeal in the purpose economy in three ways:

1 Refine your core skills.
2 Be a better listener.
3 Lead, but be open to following.

The first is to refine your *core skills* and identify the sector or organization where you can have the most impact. This means focusing in on areas where you excel and industries you know best – when you start your research, start here! What do you already know? Whose work are you already familiar with?

Second, invest in becoming a *better listener*. Think of your research in these terms: you're listening to what people are putting out there, trying to both hear and understand their needs, priorities and goals, and figuring out how they fit with you.

Case Study Tim Mohin

Tim took on a role as chief executive at GRI in Amsterdam. He spent the first three weeks of his tenure there doing what he called a listening tour; he met with his stakeholders – the people impacted by and invested in what he was doing, both external and internal – and just listened. He didn't start out by talking or sharing his wealth of knowledge. *He just listened.* This is absolutely crucial in building one of the key skills for the impact sector: empathy. The only way to have empathy is to be able to really hear and listen to what's going on with the people on the other side of the table.

Finally, sustainability professionals need to *lead* from the front, but be open to following. This is a collaborative agenda; don't worry, we'll come back to this later in Step 7.

Where the key players are

So – we know what our principles and ideals are, and we know we need to gather as much information as we can for our soft job hunt. But where can we find these key players in order to listen to them?

Inside your organization

> When personal purpose, team purpose, and organizational purpose line up, that's where real engagement is.
>
> Kevin Cashman, Senior Partner at Korn Ferry
> (Korn Ferry Institute, 2016)

Just as we touched on a second ago, a good place to start is with what you already know. In general, we're seeing sustainability teams getting bigger, with more human resource being committed to purpose agendas. Many people are being recruited from within their organizations or networks – think about it, it makes sense! If you're already within an organization, you already know the business, the stakeholders and the competitors. Most roles are filled from this 'hidden job market' – whether through an internal move or networking – whereas few are filled through a résumé search or job posting (Executive Connexions, 2018). While that might sound defeating, we're going to work through the art and science of networking in Step 13 so you can navigate this market like a pro.

It can also be difficult to figure out where impact jobs sit within organizations, because the titles change from company to company. Lines of reporting also vary greatly, with sustainability roles reporting to corporate affairs; environment, health and safety (EHS) units; marketing; legal; or finance – just to name a few. As the link between commercial performance and sustainability becomes more fully proved and accepted, sustainability-related functions will sit more and more within conventional departments – meaning that an impact-focused role might not need to sit on a purely impact-focused team. As new trends emerge around product innovation, responsible procurement, and ethical trade, look out for opportunities in design, supply chain, and marketing: candidates with education and experience in these key functions, coupled with an awareness of sustainability and knowledge of the business risks and opportunities, will be in demand.

Around the impact market

You're only going to find so many key players within your own organization, so you'll need to branch out into the broader market for inspiration, especially if you're not looking to stay with your current employer. Here are some tips for how you can find players you may not know personally:

- In Step 1, you spent some time researching the purpose economy, reading white papers, and following news feeds. What organizations came up in that process? Visit their websites, look up their staff listings to see who holds a role that interests you, and look up those people on LinkedIn.
- Think of the people you know who have impact jobs, even if their specific role isn't one you want. Look them up on LinkedIn, and take a look at their own connections. You're likely to find people in interesting roles, and you can follow that thread of connections through LinkedIn to find more people and organizations.
- As you continue to read news related to the purpose economy, pay attention whenever someone is quoted. Find that person on LinkedIn or search for their bio online.

We'll do a practical exercise with this research at the end of this step, so keep track of the people you identify.

Be an agent of change

Keep in mind that 'sustainability' doesn't need to be in your job title for you to be a sustainability practitioner. Rather, 'doing' sustainability involves creating change from within the system to move society towards your values. It can be the guiding star in almost any role, and following it takes a lot of passion and belief.

Soft skills – including the ability to communicate, motivate and facilitate – are crucial, while harder skills such as strategic planning, systems thinking, project management, and financial analysis to demonstrate viability are also important. You want to be able to provide the evidence base for change; the ability to build the business case, and to bring these issues on to everyone's agenda – especially that of the board of directors – will be critical to success.

Case Study   Dave Stangis

Dave, founder and CEO of 21C Impact, entered the field of corporate citizenship from the science and engineering field. He spent the early part of his career in operational jobs at an automotive, utility and technology manufacturing company and moved from there to creating and designing Intel's first corporate responsibility role and strategy before transitioning into his current position. Dave advises jobseekers to treat their search with urgency, but to take the long view. Dave said:

> Be the best in the job you have today, and you'll never have to worry about what's next. Listen, listen, and listen, then do your best to translate and align what you've heard to the challenge at hand. Push as hard as physically possible, but do so with tact and dexterity: your best ideas only work if others believe they are theirs.

Market opportunities – does my dream job even exist?

Now that you've explored some of the key people in the purpose economy, let's think about the possible roles you might want to target. Remember, we're going to bring all of this together in our exercise at the end of this step.

The range of opportunities in the impact space is quite diverse, and it helps to consider what sort of organization and role would be the best fit for you. Note that government is quite different from NGOs, which in turn are different from social enterprises and sustainable businesses. In the same vein, being an entrepreneur is very different from working in operations for a company.

It can be useful to think about where your ideal roles and organizations intersect, and perhaps build up your own grid to evaluate your options. We'll get very decisive and targeted about this in Step 3, our next step, but for now, consider the sustainability careers matrix (Table 2.1). Career coach Katie Kross originally published a version of this matrix in her excellent 2009 book, *Profession and Purpose*. The one I provide in Table 2.1 is reworked to reflect today's landscape, and is designed to help you think about whether you want to help a traditional company become more sustainability-oriented or to help a sustainability-oriented company to grow. Put another way: do you want to make a big company 'green', or a 'green' company big? Remember, somewhere in this impact space is a role for you with the right cultural fit, and there are various pathways you can follow to get to it.

So, are you going to choose a traditional organization, or a sustainability-focused one? Are you going to pursue a role that is sustainability-oriented, or a traditional role? Do you envision changing a big multinational company from the inside, or do you prefer working in a more nimble, start-up environment or a B Corps, which are legally required to consider the impact of their decisions on their workers, customers, suppliers, community and the environment?

TABLE 2.1 Sustainability careers matrix

		What type of role aligns with your skills?	
		Impact- or mission-focused	Business or commercial
What type of organization aligns with your values?	**Impact- or mission-focused**	Senior Manager for Corporate Responsibility at Natura Cosmeticos	Brand Marketing Manager at All Birds
		Sustainability Consultant at Quantis International	Planning & Business Development Manager at Peet's Coffee & Tea
		Head of Climate Initiatives at World Economic Forum	Accounting Specialist at Tom's Of Maine
		Global Partnership Lead at Impact Hub	Product Management Lead at IDEO
		Global Public Policy Director at Deloitte	Senior Account Director at LinkedIn
	Business or commercial	Director of Public Affairs, Sustainability & Social Innovation at Danone	Financial Analyst at Barclays
		Head of Environmental Sustainability at GlaxoSmithKline	Senior Brand Manager at Unilever
		Sustainable Innovation Senior Manager at Kering	Head of Design at IKEA

Source: Adapted from Kross, K (2009) *Profession and Purpose*

WORLD'S MOST SUSTAINABLE CORPORATIONS

Perhaps it would help to look at some examples of sustainable companies. An organization called Corporate Knights does an annual ranking of corporate sustainability performance, which they release every January at the World Economic Forum in Davos and publish in leading media outlets (Corporate Knights, 2020). They rank companies based on publicly disclosed information – such as financial filings and sustainability reports – rather than self-submissions from companies. Corporate Knights considers multiple key criteria for their ranking, including:

- energy, carbon, water, waste productivity;
- CEO to average employee pay;
- percentage tax paid;
- pension fund status;
- safety performance – lost time per injury and fatalities;
- employee turnover;
- leadership diversity;
- sustainability pay link.

Take a look at the most recent list – you should be able to find it online. Look up the leading companies and see how they're structured, what they do, and who occupies the positions that might interest you.

Case Study   Neeraj Aggarwal

Neeraj started his career in mergers and acquisitions at global investment banks such as Morgan Stanley and Rothschild, but then realized he wanted to make more of a difference, so, after his MBA, he started to focus more on the impact investing space. He wanted to leverage his Indian heritage with his time living in Australia, and he wanted real-world experience. He started working with impact investing organizations in the United Kingdom, United States, and India during his MBA, and then spent five years at the Michael & Susan Dell Foundation where he was the programme director of impact investing and of the Rebuild Texas Fund.

Neeraj advises jobseekers to follow funds and thought leaders on social media, to look to mentors for advice on what to read, and then to read extensively, being aware of the language that your target audience uses. In Neeraj's case, this meant paying close attention to how capital investing differs from impact investing and venture philanthropy or charitable giving. We'll explore those differences in detail in Step 3.

Career tracks

So, we have a list of people to research, and a much better idea about the kind of roles you might want to target. Now it's time to think about your route in. If you're making a transition into the purpose economy from a more 'mainstream' sector, your career move is likely to follow one of the following 'tracks' – updated and adapted from career coach Katie Kross' excellent 2009 book, *Profession and Purpose* – that describe commercial roles or functions:

1 strategy;
2 finance and accounting;
3 marketing;
4 operations;
5 general management.

You're probably at least vaguely familiar with these functions already; each one can translate into functions and duties that a sustainability practitioner might take on. It's important to consider what recruiters and programme managers are looking for in these tracks, what issues they view as important, and how they are framing their hiring or contracting decisions. This should help you figure out where you'll fit best in the impact space.

Strategy

If you have strategy skills, you might apply them in the impact space in these ways:

- business planning for sustainable or social enterprises;
- corporate social responsibility or risk strategy;
- organizational change;
- policy work;
- sustainable R&D investment strategy;
- leveraging sustainability for competitive advantage;
- emerging market and 'base of the pyramid' strategy.

Finance and accounting

If you are good at finance and accounting and wonder how that translates into purpose work, you can start to seek out such keywords as:

- impact investing;
- environmental, social, governance (ESG);
- SRI;
- risk management;
- assurance;
- social return on investment (SROI) analysis;
- corporate governance and reporting;
- cleantech finance;
- full-cost accounting or environmental accounting;
- community development finance.

For anything that has a financial or analytical element to it, you would be able to translate some of your experience to be relevant in the impact space.

Marketing

If you have marketing skills, there are lots of opportunities for things like brand marketing, social marketing, cause-related marketing, and 'base of the pyramid' marketing. You can also look for new market and product development for sustainable technologies, products, or services, as well as general work in internal or external communications. Many of the opportunities in the impact space are somehow related to marketing and communications, as many organizations link sustainability to their brands and reputations.

Operations

If operations are your strong suit, you can apply your skills to roles in energy management, product stewardship or lifecycle management, logistics, responsible procurement, supplier management, and supply chain optimization. This area is a little more technical, but no less important. You also could be doing operations for a smaller organization that is a B Corp – a for-profit corporation that has been certified for social and environmental performance – or similarly mission-driven.

General management

If you are skilled at management, you would be useful in the impact space in change management and team-building resource management. You might be well suited to these roles:

- social venture and non-profit management;
- sustainability visioning and organizational change;
- stakeholder engagement and community relations;
- corporate governance;
- strategic and ethical human resources practices.

Case Study   Mario Elias Gonzalez

Mario is the Responsible Business Adviser at a global cement company, CEMEX. His eight-year career started while in his bachelor's degree when he did an internship for CEMEX focused on a purpose-driven employee volunteering programme to reach host communities to offer aid in sustainability, education and infrastructure. Upon graduation he moved to a renewable energy company leading community engagement to empower local organizations in major social issues such as health, energy, education, employment and entrepreneurship. Mario says the biggest lesson from his career progression is how to line up allies both internally and externally, and to treat criticism as useful feedback and an opportunity to grow. He says that using empathy to shift mindsets is the most important practice he employs to advance his organization's social impact programmes.

The networking opportunity map

Now it's time to pull all of this research together. The networking opportunity map below is a tool for beginning a 'soft job search', where you start mapping out who you know in the market who might be able to help you get a job, or who might know someone else who can. It will also help you to identify people who are sitting in your dream jobs or working in the space you want to be in or in the organizations you might want to be working for, and to tease out what they're doing right.

We will do more work with this map throughout the book, so it's a good idea to take some time now to do your research and begin filling it out.

NETWORKING OPPORTUNITY MAP

Identify 10 target companies or organizations for your search and fill in their details in Table 2.2. For Table 2.3, go on LinkedIn to find 10 people who are doing what you think is your dream job. Pay attention to the keywords they use in their profile, and note those down in the table.

TABLE 2.2 Top 10 target companies

 Ten companies |Target list

Company name	Location	Contact name	Contact email	Contact phone	Additional notes

TABLE 2.3   Top 10 people you want to be when you grow up

NETWORKING OPPORTUNITY MAP

Ten people | Who do you want to be when you grow up?

Contact name	Email	Title	Company	Key words from profile	Additional notes

> **KEY POINTS**
>
> In this chapter, we learned about:
>
> - how to identify the key players in the purpose economy;
> - how to identify market opportunities in the impact space;
> - career tracks for the purpose economy; and
> - mapping your network opportunities.

What's next?

In the next chapter, we will be launching into Step 3, where we will learn how to narrow the net and figure out what you want out of a dream job.

References and further reading

Corporate Knights (2020) [accessed 27 February 2020] *2020 Global 100* [Online] https://www.corporateknights.com/reports/2020-global-100/ (archived at https://perma.cc/A5PY-2UDQ)

Executive Connexions (2018) [accessed 26 March 2020] *The Executive Job Search: Navigating the hidden job market* [Online] https://www.executiveconnexions.com/the-hidden-jobs-market/ (archived at https://perma.cc/2D53-DMP8)

FindLaw Attorney Writers (2016) [accessed 25 October 2019] *Movie Day at the Supreme Court or 'I Know It When I See It': A history of the definition of obscenity* [Online] https://corporate.findlaw.com/ litigation-disputes/movie-day-at-the-supreme-court-or-i-know-it-when-i-see-it-a.html (archived at https://perma.cc/GTH3-PBQ4)

Houde, S (2014) [accessed 8 September 2020] What do sustainability and porn have in common?, *Triple Pundit* [Online] available at https://www.triplepundit.com/story/2014/sustainability-jobs-101-what-do-sustainability-and-porn-have-common/46256 (archived at https://perma.cc/29AZ-C3PU)

Korn Ferry Institute (2016) [accessed 28 October 2019] *Real World Leadership: Lead with purpose and sustain superior results* [Online] https://www.kornferry.com/media/sidebar_downloads/Korn-Ferry-Institute_RealWorldLeadership_Report-4.pdf (archived at https://perma.cc/YL2L-2MJ9)

Kross, K (2009) *Profession and Purpose: A resource guide for MBA careers in sustainability,* Greenleaf Publishing, Sheffield

PART TWO

Aim your compass

Narrowing the net

How do I figure out where I fit into the sustainability market?

Now that we've got a better understanding of the people, industries and sectors that make up the purpose economy, it's time to figure out where you fit into it. You only need one dream job to give you true purpose, right? You aren't asking for too much. But the slog, the process, the setbacks and the time investment can be killers. It can be enough to make you want to stay unfulfilled and broke until the end of time. But fear not: we're in this together, and we're going to get you the tools and strategies you need to reach your goals.

This step on narrowing the net is the most crucial of the entire career change process. If we haven't identified our target audience, market, or sector, we can't develop a compelling and relevant personal brand and positioning strategy to beat out the other 200 people in line for the same role. Getting focused early on yields results, because all the other job search tools we build later in this process – networking, job searching, cover letter writing, crafting LinkedIn profiles and résumés, and more – can be properly targeted and customized. You will map your key criteria into a one-pager, narrowing key elements down by category and then prioritizing them. The tools in this chapter – the Dream Job Targeting Tool and the Impact Career Onion – force you to make decisions about what is important to you in a pragmatic way.

TIP   Focus!

A common approach for jobseekers is to keep their options wide open to any sector and any role. This might feel like it makes sense… but it's a mistake! Casting a wide net doesn't work, especially today. You only get one LinkedIn profile, so you can't keep reinventing yourself for each application.

Why this step is important

It might seem counterintuitive to be narrowly focused in your job search. Surely, keeping an open mind means your odds of finding a job go up – isn't that just maths? But in order to be a competitive candidate, jobseekers need a targeted, specific, clear niche, especially in the purpose economy. We need to let go of the fear of focusing and narrowing our target. Pushing through this fear does not shut out opportunities – rather, it opens up relevant ones more quickly for four reasons:

1 We will have a clearer message when networking about how each person can help us. We need to make it easy for them to put us in touch with new contacts in the purpose economy by being as specific as possible. If we are too broad, they'll be overwhelmed.
2 Hiring managers want to see that you want exactly what they're offering, and that what you're selling closely matches their impact criteria.

3 Recruiters rely heavily on keyword searches on social media, so you need to narrow down your keywords to be spot on for the sustainability role you hope to land.

4 LinkedIn profiles only give you one chance. This means you can't reinvent yourself for every job or opportunity. You get to choose one brand and stick with it.

Case Study   Emilie Goodall

Emilie is the director of Impact+ at Bridges Ventures. She came from the non-governmental organization (NGO) side, starting her career as an analyst and then consultant at New Philanthropy Capital. Emilie subsequently moved to CAF Venturesome, running their development fund and leading on impact analysis. From there, she became the founder manager at the Principles for Investors in Inclusive Finance within the United Nations Principles for Responsible Investment, where she ended up supporting investors across all asset classes in their efforts to implement responsible investment practices.

Reflecting on her career trajectory, Emilie says, 'Just saying you want to do something more meaningful is not enough. Be really clear about what role you want.'

The Impact Career Onion

Let's peel back the Impact Career Onion (Figure 3.1) to get a better idea of how to target our thinking.

The onion has five layers. First, you need to decide if you want to be playing on the global field or at the local level. You may want to be on the ground in an emerging market working in impact investing or international development, two tracks that will require global focus and experience. But there are also many grassroots opportunities and smaller B Corps that may not be global... yet.

FIGURE 3.1   Impact Career Onion

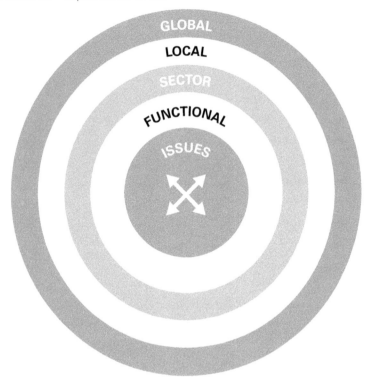

On the other hand, you may not be able to travel or live abroad, so having a more local impact makes more sense. You may also feel that you can have the most impact and be most able to see the outcome of your work at a local level. There are no right or wrong answers here; it's just a matter of figuring out what's important to you.

Once you've established whether you want to focus on global or local work, the next three layers of the onion contemplate your sector, function and issues.

Sector

Let's take a closer look at your sector. A sector is an area of the economy in which organizations share common operating characteristics. In the impact economy, we first need to decide whether we want to work in the public sector, in the private sector, or for an NGO (non-governmental organization).

For the purposes of our Impact Career Onion exercise, think of sector as the *way you deliver impact*. Is it through private business, governmental regulation and policy, or non-profit work that's generally donor-funded?

It's important to make a choice, not least because the language and style of your applications will need to vary greatly between these three sectors. For instance, the private sector may talk about 'business development', while an NGO would call the same thing 'corporate partnerships' or 'fundraising', whereas in the public sector it may be more about 'grant giving'.

Another aspect of defining your sector is to consider the industry in which you want to work, or on which you hope to have an impact. An industry is a group of companies that are related based on their primary business activities. You can see some industry examples in Figure 3.2. For the purposes of our Impact Career Onion exercise, think of industry as the *space in which you deliver impact.*

Think about what industries you have already worked in or know well, and then which ones you have worked with in some capacity, perhaps as a client, partner, or regulator. Being explicit about your knowledge of specific industries is crucial to proving your understanding of the organization's stakeholders, products, or risks.

PRIVATE SECTOR

If you decide that the private sector is where you want to be, you need to choose between in-house practitioner roles and

FIGURE 3.2   Impact Career Onion – sector

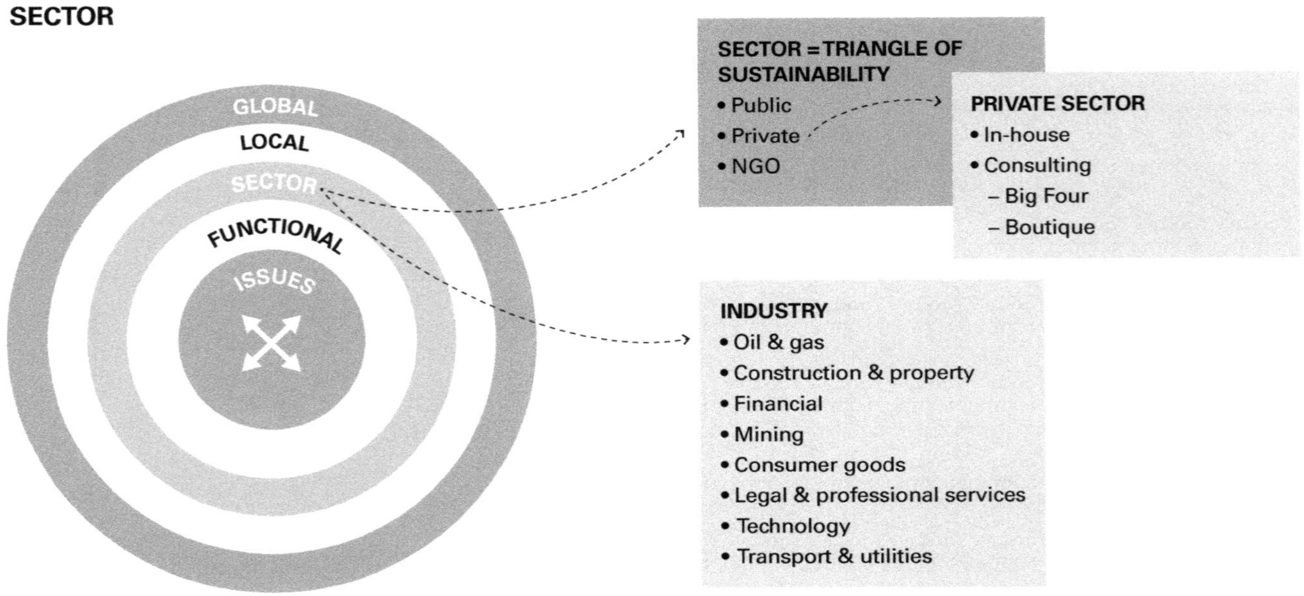

SECTOR

SECTOR = TRIANGLE OF SUSTAINABILITY
- Public
- Private
- NGO

PRIVATE SECTOR
- In-house
- Consulting
  - Big Four
  - Boutique

INDUSTRY
- Oil & gas
- Construction & property
- Financial
- Mining
- Consumer goods
- Legal & professional services
- Technology
- Transport & utilities

GLOBAL

LOCAL

SECTOR

FUNCTIONAL

ISSUES

consulting roles. If you pick the consulting pathway, you then need to think about whether one of the 'Big Four' consultancies or a smaller boutique will be a better cultural fit for you.

Consulting pathway vs in-house pathway
Many people who want to break into the sustainability field struggle to focus on the type of role that would fit them best. When I have clients who say they could see themselves working in consulting, in-house or for a non-profit, that raises a red flag for me, because those are all very different cultures and offer very different roles within them, not to mention very different business drivers. If you're trying to decide what is the best focus for you, here are important ways that sustainability consulting is very different from in-house positions:

Competitiveness: Consulting is extremely competitive! It's important to hone your networking skills if you want to go down this pathway, because you will need contacts. Consulting also situates you as an outsider on the client team, which means you need to be likeable and persuasive in order to gain trust. In-house roles are less competitive than consulting because there are more of them in the market and there is also more variety to the types of roles you may find depending on the sector, industry and where the company is on the sustainability journey. Both types of pathway will require that you promote yourself effectively in the job application process so that you are relevant and compelling, ie competitive.

Pay: Contrary to what you may think, consultants are paid less than in-house staff, even though consulting is a high-pressure, client-facing occupation. Boutiques like SustainAbility (now owned by ERM), Salter Baxter, and BSR pay even less than the 'Big Four' consultancies we discussed in Step 1. Various salary surveys by GreenBiz and Acre over the years have found substantial differences in pay, with consultants earning tens of thousands less than in-house staff every year.

Remember that it takes one month of job searching and preparation for every $10,000 you want to earn.

Hours: Consultants I have worked with, in general, complain of longer and less predictable hours than their in-house counterparts. This is due to the client-facing nature of project work. If a potential client calls on a Friday afternoon and wants a proposal for new work on Tuesday, you may have to work through the weekend. Everything in consulting is time-sensitive and externally driven by client needs and expectations. This can lead to quite unpredictable hours requiring undying flexibility. While in-house roles are demanding in their own right, they have more stable hours.

Strategy vs implementation: As a consultant, you won't typically be able to see projects through to the end. Generally, you'll step away long before the initiative is in full swing, meaning that you won't be around to see the impact of the project. You'll need instead to derive satisfaction from the intrinsic value of your work, and of the variation of projects, impact issues and clients, without necessarily reaping the satisfaction of its successful outcome. As an in-house practitioner, you take a strategy all the way through to implementation – but you may also need to negotiate internal buy-in from senior leaders, and influence cross-functional teams to go on the journey with you.

Diversity of sector: The good news is that consulting positions allow you to work on a variety of projects, in different sectors, with diverse clients. Some larger consultancies, like the Big Four, may be structured by sector. But in the smaller boutiques, a consultant could be working across multiple sectors, making it a dynamic way to experience multiple types of businesses. If you are in-house, you will likely be an expert not only in your sector, but also in your specific commercial business. You will need to know the business and its stakeholders inside and out, which is why many in-house sustainability practitioners are internal hires.

As a consultant, you must be able to build business, work with clients, and grow new leads. You will likely have a numerical target to bring in business, especially as you get more senior. Here are some of the skills you need to land a consulting role:

- thrive under pressure;
- build client relations;
- grow new business development/sales;
- write proposals;
- pitch to potential clients.

For in-house roles, these are some of the skills that are in demand:

- implement projects from start to finish;
- measure long-term impacts;
- collaborate cross-functionally;
- build partnerships internally and externally;
- represent the organization externally;
- design policies to embed strategies.

Finally, there are some skills that are necessary in both consultant and in-house roles:

- turn the United Nations Sustainable Development Goals into strategic frameworks;
- be strategic in spotting sustainability market opportunities;
- manage projects, budgets and teams;
- influence, negotiate and persuade at a senior level;
- design presentations using PowerPoint;
- speak publicly about strategic frameworks;
- listen and empathize.

NGO OR PUBLIC SECTOR

If you decide you want to go into the non-profit/NGO space or the public/government sector, you will need to be aware that the drivers are very different than in the for-profit world, where shareholder returns, bottom-line profits and efficiencies usually underpin operations. In the NGO or public sector, you will most likely find that there is less innovation, a slower pace, and more bureaucracy. The focus may be more on policy, advocacy, or shifting mindsets, rather than making margins on products or services. Those priorities will drive the workplace culture, too. In an NGO, you may feel closer to the on-the-ground impact of your work. Similarly, in the public sector you're likely to feel more able to shape change at a local or national level through legislation and regulations.

When I graduated from my MBA, I landed my first management job at World Wide Fund for Nature (WWF) in the international headquarters in Gland, Switzerland, just outside of Geneva. I was thrilled to be able to go to work every day and feel I was making a difference to the oceans, wildlife, forests and climate across the globe. However, I quickly realized that my corporate mindset of fast-moving, efficient systems and processes didn't align well with NGO culture. I loved getting to travel to Kenya and see the wildlife we were saving, but at the end of the day my style and pace of innovation and work ethic just weren't a good fit for the NGO sector. I went back to corporate but as a consultant at the intersection of the two sectors, managing the community investment programmes between companies and their NGO partners.

Job postings often aren't explicit about their sector-related requirements, so it's good practice to map the employer's clients, suppliers, or stakeholders to get a solid understanding of the sectors they serve or engage.

Function

In evaluating your functional pathway (Figure 3.3), we're really just talking about skills and tasks: what will you be doing on a day-to-day basis?

FIGURE 3.3 Impact career sector – function

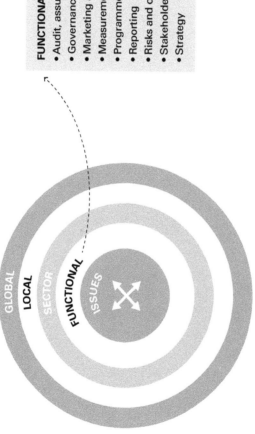

FUNCTIONAL = SKILLS BASED
- Audit, assurance
- Governance and policies
- Marketing and communications
- Measurement
- Programme/project management
- Reporting
- Risks and opportunities
- Stakeholder engagement
- Strategy

GLOBAL

LOCAL

SECTOR

FUNCTIONAL

ISSUES

Examples of functional requirements in sustainability job listings include reporting and transparency, environmental and social policy, stakeholder engagement, and risk identification and management, just to name a few. We will work through this more in Step 7, when we focus on mapping and proving your skills, but for now, it's worth just reflecting on the work functions you're good at, the ones you enjoy, and those you want to focus on.

Issues

This layer of the onion deals with your in-depth knowledge of a specific area (Figure 3.4). It's important that you decide which two or three issues you will stake out as your focus.

Once you narrow down your focus issues, you'll need to make sure to communicate these in your personal marketing tools, as recruiters will search on keywords that are associated with those issues. So, if you settle on renewable energy as your issue, and you work in the solar industry, make sure to use both terms so that you cover all the keywords for searchability.

If we parse the issues in the purpose economy, they generally fall into four core categories: environment, community, workplace, and marketplace. Consider these examples as a starting point, but not at all a complete list:

Environment

- climate change and greenhouse gas emissions;
- regulatory and legislative compliance;
- water use;
- waste management and recycling;
- transport emissions;
- environmental management systems.

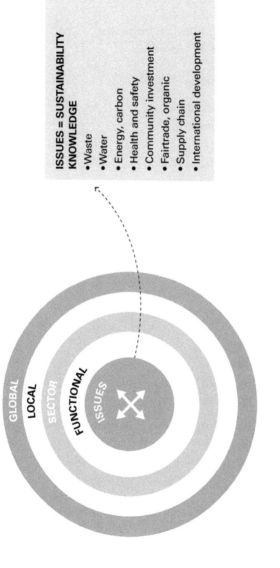

FIGURE 3.4   Impact career sector – issues

Community

- cash, time, or in-kind donations;
- community/charity partnerships;
- employee volunteering;
- community and business benefits;
- corporate philanthropy.

Workplace (internal stakeholders)

- employee engagement;
- health and safety;
- human rights;
- diversity and inclusion;
- training and development.

Marketplace (external stakeholders)

- responsible sourcing;
- supply chain;
- privacy;
- consumer rights;
- ethical trade.

EXERCISE   Match purpose economy issues to the UN Sustainable Development Goals

In Step 1, we discussed the United Nations Sustainable Development Goals (SDGs), noting that they increasingly inform corporate, NGO, and government sustainability strategies. Take a moment here to consider how the issues listed above match up to one or more of the 17 SDGs in Figure 3.5. The better you understand this impact ecosystem, the more successful you'll be at finding your place within it.

FIGURE 3.5 UN SDGs

SUSTAINABLE DEVELOPMENT GALS

1 NO POVERTY

2 ZERO HUNGER

3 GOOD HEALTH AND WELL BEING

4 QUALITY EDUCATION

5 GENDER EQUALITY

6 CLEAN WATER AND SANITATION

7 AFFORDABLE AND CLEAN ENERGY

8 DECENT WORK AND ECONOMIC GROWTH

9 INDUSTRY, INNOVATION AND INFRASTRUCTURE

10 REDUCED INEQUALITIES

11 SUSTAINABLE CITIES AND COMMUNITIES

12 RESPONSIBLE CONSUMPTION AND PRODUCTION

13 CLIMATE ACTION

14 LIFE BELOW WATER

15 LIFE ON LAND

16 PEACE, JUSTICE AND STRONG INSTITUTIONS

17 PARTNERSHIPS FOR THE GOALS

If you're like most of my clients – and me, for that matter! – you may say that all these issues interest you. That's really common among people who want to work in the purpose economy, and it's part of what makes this space so wonderful. But homing in on two or three issues within one of these categories will help you to build a more specialized and relevant story. The more specific you are, the better.

> **TIP**
>
> Don't try to change too many things at once. If you take the layers of the onion and just change one layer at a time, you will greatly increase your chances of making a successful career change. If you really want to change your location, role, *and* sector, consider taking a role that just changes one of the layers at a time, before making a bigger jump a few years later.

Examples of career tracks

Following are some examples of career tracks within the purpose economy, and some details on how to navigate them.

Social enterprise track

Social entrepreneurship is thriving, but what does it take to launch a social enterprise successfully? It's helpful to think of a social enterprise as a hybrid of a start-up and an NGO. If you want to use your skills to break out on your own and kick-start an innovative business that will make a difference to the world, you'll need certain attributes to succeed. Social entrepreneurs are unique: they identify a problem and use entrepreneurial principles to organize, create and manage a venture in order to yield positive returns to both society and the bottom line. So, what are the most important skills of a social entrepreneur?

VISION

You'll need a robust and diverse skillset that will enable you to switch between your marketing hat, your finance hat, and your legal hat quickly and smoothly. You may feel like a bit of a mad hatter at times, but this is also what makes a social entrepreneur tick. To succeed, you'll need a strong, clear vision – the message that you communicate to your partners, your team, and your clients – that sets your company apart from other mainstream businesses in the same sector. Successful social entrepreneurs are those who use their particular strengths to address a gap in the market and solve a big social problem.

COMMITMENT

A social entrepreneur is driven by passion and dedication to see a project through to the bitter end. You'll need an intense focus on your goals and strategies if you're to achieve your ambitions. Nurture that fire in your belly! Be ready for the long hours and the ups and downs that will challenge you. Get a support network in place now so that you have champions to help you stay the course.

WILLINGNESS TO LEARN

Your intuition is your friend in this game, but know when it's telling you to gather evidence! Acknowledging the gaps in your knowledge will increase your resilience, both in terms of your business and your capacity to solve the social problem you've identified. Be a sponge, absorb knowledge and ask questions. Get help when you need it. Your core competencies may not be enough to cover the full scope of your enterprise's needs, so get a good network of colleagues to help you grow and learn on your journey.

REALISM

If your background is in journalism, don't try to set up a restaurant. Straying too far from the industry you know will put your social enterprise on shaky ground from the start. Rather, work from your strengths, and keep your project real and your business model solid. You'll be competing against conventional businesses and the consumer won't compromise on quality for the sake of a social conscience. Be sure that your social agenda only *adds* value; don't make it a substitute for a good product.

RESEARCH

The resources available to social entrepreneurs are growing by the day, so you'll definitely need to do your due diligence to understand the space and how your proposition fits into it. Here are just a few sources to check as you develop your business plan:

- *Crunchbase* is a platform for finding business information about private and public companies, including early-stage start-ups. You can use it to get a sense of who's getting funded, get insights into the competition, identify industry trends, and more.
- *Columbia Business School's Tamer Center for Social Enterprise* trains the next generation of social entrepreneurs. Its website features a wealth of research, news, profiles and events in the social enterprise space.
- *Ashoka* nurtures a community of change leaders and runs a fellowship programme for social entrepreneurs. Its 'Changemaker Network' is extensive.

Investment track

If you are looking to move into investing for positive social or environmental outcomes, we can use our Impact Career Onion tool again, but with a few adjustments. When we're on the sectors and markets layer, we specifically want to evaluate knowledge or impact areas. You can see some examples in our modified onion (Figure 3.6).

FIGURE 3.6   Peeling the investing onion

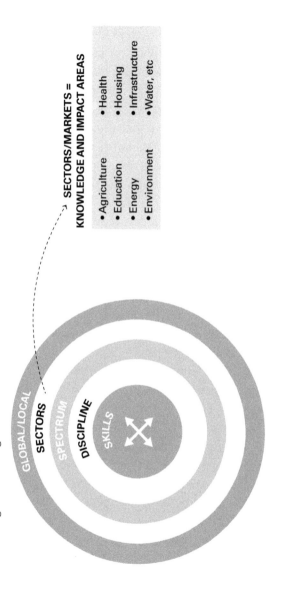

GLOBAL/LOCAL

SECTORS

SPECTRUM

DISCIPLINE

SKILLS

SECTORS/MARKETS =
KNOWLEDGE AND IMPACT AREAS

- Agriculture
- Education
- Energy
- Environment
- Health
- Housing
- Infrastructure
- Water, etc

After that, we need to decide where you want to sit on the investment spectrum, which includes sustainable investing and impact investing. These are very different worlds with significant differences between them, so it's a good idea to figure out and target where you want to live on this spectrum. Notice that the illustration in Figure 3.7 also includes philanthropy. You'll see that these categories differ in two important ways: whether they are designed to generate financial returns, and whether they are intended to produce positive social or environmental results.

Next, we turn to the discipline layer, where you consider the type of organization that interests you. Do you want to work with a fund in money management? Are you more inclined toward investment management and deal structuring? Or are you best suited to a financial advisory?

The expanding investment space comprises foundations, venture philanthropists, non-profits, technical assistance providers, financial institutions, and a growing number of major corporations. The Global Impact Investing Network (GIIN) and the Aspen Network of Development Entrepreneurs (ANDE) membership lists are both great places to learn about the players and companies in this space.

Figure 3.8 provides a great overview of the space and how the different disciplines interact. Find yourself on it and focus on that area.

We've now reached the centre of our onion where we need to evaluate your sector-specific skills. In general, you'll need strong industry understanding, including impact measurement models, a sharp intellect, and the ability to speak the language of investment banking. Experience in investing or with specific impact areas helps. Here are some of the skills that you are likely to need in the investing space:

- engaging stakeholders;
- mapping the landscape of customers, employees, suppliers, investors, community and environment;

FIGURE 3.7 The spectrum of investors, capital and enterprises

CAPITAL INVESTING			IMPACT INVESTING		PHILANTHROPY	
Investing that deploys capital with the anticipation of generating financial returns to the investor but **no expectation** of generating positive social and/or environmental impact.			Socially motivated investing that deploys capital with the anticipation of generating financial returns to the investor **alongside** positive social and/or environmental impact.		Socially motivated funding that deploys capital with the anticipation of generating positive social and/or environmental impact for society but no financial returns to the funder.	
SOCIALLY NEUTRAL INVESTING						
Mainstream Investing	**Socially Responsible Investing (SRI)**	**Sustainable Investing (ESG)**	**Non-Concessionary Impact Investing**	**Concessionary Impact Investing**	**Venture Philanthropy**	**Charitable Giving**
Investing in companies without consideration of social or environmental impact	Using a negative investing screen to **exclude** companies considered ethically problematic	Using a positive investing screen to **include** the environmental, social, and governance (ESG) considerations of companies	Investing that seeks measurable social impact alongside risk-adjusted financial returns	Investing that is willing to make some financial sacrifice – either taking greater risks or accepting lower returns – to achieve social goals	Funding non-profit social enterprises that generate some or all of their revenues from business activities	Funding non-profit social enterprises that rely completely on charitable donations

FIGURE 3.8   The investment players flow chart

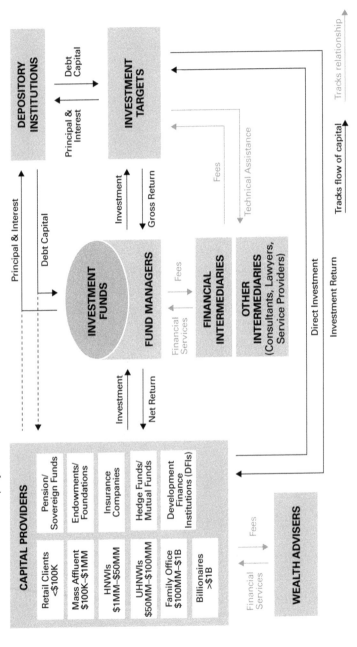

- discovering opportunities;
- modelling the future and interpreting the past;
- synthesizing ideas for metrics, measurement, analysis, or conversion;
- finance and accounting;
- deciding to invest or not;
- analytic rigor;
- spreadsheet/Excel modelling for how investments could succeed;
- measuring the impact, income, risk and return potential.

The investing track is an extremely competitive one, and it's hard to break in if you don't know where you fit on the spectrum. That said, this area offers plenty of room to differentiate your work, with many different angles to pursue across a broad landscape of social and environmental issues. You can stand out by bringing new ideas for metrics, measurement, analysis, or conversion.

International/sustainable development track

Many of my clients want to break into international/sustainable development. This track presents important pros and cons.

The bad news is that it's extremely competitive. It's also really hard. Many people glamourize this field, but it's definitely not for everyone. It can be uncomfortable and even dangerous. You have to be prepared to fail a lot. This can be a frustrating career, and you won't make a ton of money doing it.

On the positive side, the development community is small and tightly knit. Once you're in, you're in, and you can move up quickly. At its best, it's also deeply rewarding. Development is a labour of love that pays off in ways you can't even imagine now.

To be successful in international/sustainable development, you'll generally need dedication, in-country experience, an advanced degree, a thick skin and foreign languages.

Dream job targeting

Now that we've peeled our onion – hopefully without too many tears! – let's turn to mapping your dream job criteria. This is the key tool for Step 3. It's your chance to dream about key criteria for a meaningful career.

In Table 3.1, mark 'No', 'Yes', or 'Please' against aspects of your past and current jobs. The aim is to end up with a one-page map, to keep your career path on target. Remember: having too many tracks or interests works against you in the job market, so the more focused you are, the better and faster results you will have in your search. As you're completing this exercise, keep the following in mind:

1 List words, not sentences.
2 Focus on the YES column, as these are the areas where you have an exact match and proved experience.
3 In the 'Yes' and 'Please' columns, put an E next to two or three essential aspects, and a D next to two or three desired aspects.
4 Highlight any items that you think require development activities.

As you can see, there is a 'Target Criteria' column on the left, and 'No/Yes/Please' columns on the right. The 'No' column is a placeholder for the things you know you don't want, a kind of mental parking space. Once the negative aspects are in there, we can ignore them and move on without the risk of them tainting the positive elements.

Then we jump to the most important column – the 'Yes' column – which asks about any prior experience on which you want to keep building. If you're a career switcher, you can draw from blogs, social media, volunteer experience, college projects – anything, really, as long as you're going to be positioning it later on a CV/résumé.

The E and D stand for essential and desired. You may have many different options and interests in your head; if you tend to get overwhelmed by all the different pathways you could take that might make you happy, this column is to help you prioritize.

Case Study   Hannah Green

Hannah landed an in-house corporate role at British healthcare firm Bupa from a background in charity work via an interim role in the private sector at Sky. She then used her Bupa experience to move to GlaxoSmithKline, the pharmaceutical company, where she took the role of Corporate Responsibility Engagement Manager and was then quickly promoted to the role of Director of Corporate Responsibility, proving that taking a side step to get into the right company is worth it.

Hannah says: 'The Dream Job Targeting Tool helped me to break down each aspect of my position that I wanted to change (like my industry, role, and location) and which aspects I wanted to keep (like my issues expertise). It helped me define what I wanted to get me focused and clear about who I would target.'

In my coaching work, I hear one question (or variations thereof) from so many jobseekers: I have applied to more than 30 jobs and have had no positive responses. What am I doing wrong?

When this happens, jobseekers are almost always casting their nets too wide. When you narrow your target focus, you will get more results, be more relevant to your audience's language, and be more pointed in your networking. This is a numbers game to some extent, but it's not about spraying the market with applications and hoping they see your value. Your task is to show them your value from the very beginning. Fewer and better-quality applications will be your new strategy.

To get this right, take your time with your dream job targeting, and be thorough and contemplative in your efforts to fill it

TABLE 3.1 Dream job targeting

TARGET CRITERIA	NO: What aspects of your current (or past) experience/job do you NOT want in your future position?	YES: What aspects of your current (or past) experience/job do you want to KEEP in a future position?	PLEASE: What aspects of a future job have you NOT HAD YET and want in your future position?
Sector: NGO, corporate*, international development, government, academic, social enterprise, etc (PICK 1)			
*Sector – Part B: If you picked corporate just above, then drill down one more level to decide 1 – in-house or 2 – consulting (PICK 1)			
Industry: Financial services, Consumer goods, Property, Mining, Retail, Oil and Gas, etc (PICK 2)			

Impact Issues/expertise/ knowledge: Waste, water, renewable energy, carbon, health & safety, human rights, fairtrade, supply chain, financial inclusion, etc (PICK 3)		
Office: Environment, Culture, Management, Team, People, etc		
Other: Commute, Logistics, Salary, Hours, etc		

out completely before moving on to the next step. This will be the bedrock of everything that comes next in our process of finding you the job that allows you to fulfil your purpose.

KEY POINTS

In this chapter, we learned about:

- where you fit into the sustainability jobs market;
- the Impact Career Onion; and
- how to target your dream job.

What's next?

In the next chapter we'll be launching into Step 4, where we will learn about the two-way street of values-based organizations and how to match your values and traits to theirs.

The two-way street of values-based organizations

How do I match my values and traits to theirs?

Hopefully you've made some progress in figuring out where you fit into the purpose economy. Now let's work on shaping the language of your personal brand, a framework for how you will describe yourself. This step is designed to help you reach a better understanding of what is important to you, so that you can align your career with your core values more effectively. Remember: both you and the prospective employers you encounter are shopping for the right fit. As jobseekers, we can often feel that we're on the back foot, and that the hiring managers are the ones with all the power… but the match needs to work for *both* parties.

Why this step is important

What do sustainability hiring managers really want to know? Their evaluation of you boils down to four key questions:

- *Do you fit the culture, team, and mission of the organization?*
  Translation – What are your **values**?
- *Do I want to work with you?*
  Translation – What are your **traits**?
- *Can you do the job?*
  Translation – What are your **skills**?
- *What are you an expert in?*
  Translation – What are your **impact issues**, and in what areas do you have **specialized knowledge?**

We already addressed knowledge and impact issues in Step 3 when we did our dream job targeting, and we'll cover skills in more detail when we get to Step 7. Now let's look at values and traits.

Values are the principles and priorities that help us make decisions every day. Values don't typically change throughout our lives, as they are strongly linked to our sense of who we are. As adults, we have developed a handful of core values that guide our decision-making and life choices.

Understanding our values is important in any type of job search, but it's absolutely critical for people working in the impact sector, as the impact sector is a values-driven space. You will feel a lot more grounded and happy when you recognize and identify your values, and when you commit to staying true to them. If you don't stay true to your values, you will feel an internal conflict, an uneasiness, and things just will feel wrong. This can be a significant source of unhappiness. For instance, if you value family but have to work 60 hours a week and travel, like in consulting work, you will feel internal stress and conflict. Similarly, if you don't value perfectionism but you work in an environment of micromanagers, you are likely to get very frustrated with your job and your boss.

This is why prioritizing to articulate your values is so crucial as one of our first steps. Values determine your priorities; they underpin and drive all of your actions. At a deeper level, they're also the measures you use to gauge whether your life has purpose. You will feel aligned and in flow when others around you share your values, so it is important to make sure your next boss, team and employer are as aligned as possible.

Following on from our values, **traits** are descriptive qualities or characteristics of a person. Like values, they are also typically core to our sense of who we are. Our traits are adjectives for how someone else would describe us – how we deliver on a task, our style of working, our approach. They will also help us to define our unique selling points for the impact sector, a concept we will revisit in further detail as we move through the steps.

In this step, you're aiming to prioritize your values and traits into a concise list. In doing so, you will:

- gain clarity about and focus on what is most important to you;
- make consistent decisions in your sustainability job search;
- take committed action to make a difference in the world while staying true to yourself;
- intelligently connect your values to your impact goals; and
- improve the results you get in the areas that are most important to you.

EXERCISE   Digging into your values

Answer the following questions off the top of your head. You may need to come back to them later, which is fine. Please try to think of tangible and specific examples from your career and your personal life so that you show a balanced view.

Step 1: Think of a time when you felt most grounded and in flow.

- Where were you? _____

   _____

- What tasks were you doing? _____

   _____

- Who were you with? _____
  _____

- What else enabled you to feel a sense of purpose? _____
  _____

Step 2: Think of a time when you were most proud of an achievement.

- What felt good about achieving your goal? _____
  _____

- Who else recognized you and your achievement? _____
  _____

- What else contributed to your sense of pride? _____
  _____

Step 3: Think of a time when you were most aligned to your purpose.

- What were you working on or doing? _____
  _____

- Who were you helping or engaging with? _____
  _____

- What else enabled you to feel a sense of purpose? _____
  _____

Defining your values and traits

Now let's work towards a definition of your values and traits in your own words.

Step 1

From the list of professional and personal values below, first tick or highlight all the words that appeal to you. This is by no means a comprehensive list, so feel free to add any values of your own. Lots of people initially look at the list and feel that many or even most of the values resonate with them: that's alright, we'll narrow things down as we go along. You'll also notice that some of these overlap in their definitions, and that's fine too.

Accountability	Discipline
Accuracy	Discovery
Adaptability	Ease of use
Adventure	Ecological awareness
Aliveness, vitality	Economic security
All for one and one for all	Effectiveness
Authenticity	Efficiency
Autonomy	Equality
Being around open and	Ethical practice
tolerant people	Excellence
Calm, quietude, peace	Excitement
Challenge	Fairness
Change and variety	Faith
Close relationships	Fame
Collaboration	Family
Commitment	Fast pace
Communication	Financial gain
Community	Flair
Compassion	Flexible work schedule
Competence	Freedom
Competition	Friendship
Concern for others	Fun
Content over form	Generosity
Continuous improvement	Global view
Cooperation	Good will
Coordination	Goodness
Creativity	Grace
Cross-cultural awareness	Gratitude
Customer satisfaction	Growth
Decisiveness	Happiness
Delight of being, joy	Hard work
Democracy	Harmony

Honesty

Honour

Humour

Inclusivity

Independence

Influencing others

Innovation

Integrity

Intentionality

Involvement

Justice

Knowledge

Leadership

Learning

Loyalty

Meaning

Merit

Money

Nature

Openness

Order

Peace, non-violence

Perfection

Perseverance

Personal development

Pleasure

Positive attitude

Power

Practicality

Preservation

Privacy

Problem-solving

Progress

Prosperity, wealth

Punctuality

Purpose

Quality of work

Recognition

Resilience

Resourcefulness

Respect for others

Responsiveness

Results-oriented

Rule of law

Safety

Satisfying others

Security

Self-reliance

Service to others, society

Simplicity

Skill

Speed

Spirit

Stability

Standardization

Status

Stewardship

Systemization

Teamwork

Timeliness

Tolerance

Tradition

Tranquillity

Trust

Truth

Unity

Variety

Wisdom

Step 2

Now that you've highlighted the values that resonate with you, go back and prioritize your top 10. You may find this part more challenging, so this could be a good moment to take a break and have a mindful moment of reflection to get a bit of perspective before you proceed. Think about which of these values have truly guided your behaviour and shaped your life. Compare values with each other – if you had to choose one over the other, which would come first? When you're ready, write down your top 10 values here.

_____

_____

_____

_____

_____

_____

_____

_____

_____

_____

Step 3

Now it's time to refine things even further, and to bring your traits into the picture alongside your values. Some of the values from the list above may also be used to describe you or your traits. Take the 10 words you chose above and drop them into the boxes at the bottom of Table 4.1. Just remember that values are nouns, and they define something you want in your next job. Traits are adjectives, and they describe you or your style of working. The important differences are provided in the table as a guide.

TABLE 4.1   Values and traits worksheet

	Values	Traits
Definition	Principles or standards of behaviour; your judgement of what is important in life	A descriptive quality or characteristic
Hiring manager question	*Do you fit our culture, team and mission?*	*Do I want to work with you? Do I want to manage you?*
Summary	What do you expect from your work culture, context and colleagues? What are your **external expectations?**	How would someone else describe you? What is your **unique selling point?**
YOUR 5:		
1		
2		
3		
4		
5		

The words you list in Table 4.1 will ultimately end up at the top of your CV (Step 8), so choose words that you would want to communicate externally to a professional audience in the impact sector.

VALUES AND TRAITS EXAMPLES

Below you'll see some examples of individual values and traits. Note how they use distinct words for each: you don't want your values and traits to say the same thing about you. For instance, you wouldn't want to list 'innovation' as one of your values and 'innovative' as one of your traits.

Example 1

Values	Traits
Innovation	Organized
Partnership	Proactive
Accountability	Entrepreneurial
Personal development	Communicative
Adaptability	Positive
	Decisive

Example 2

Values	Traits
Challenge	Diplomatic
Intellectual stimulation	Personable
Sense of purpose	Reliable
Recognition	Perceptive
Development	Calm
	Positive

Example 3

Values	Traits
Excellence	Committed
Environmental and social integrity	Optimistic
Openness	Tenacious
Energy	Calm under pressure
	Industrious

Example 4

Values	Traits
Ethical excellence	Entrepreneurial
Innovation	Strategic
Achievement	Dynamic
Pragmatism	Creative
Challenge	Good-humoured
Excitement	Motivating

Example 5

Values	Traits
Straightforward communication	Non-conforming
Positive business impact on society	Respectful
	Entrepreneurial
	Self-motivated
	Persuasive

Example 6

Values	Traits
Accountability	Innovative
Overcoming challenges	Entrepreneurial
Helping others	Driven
Efficiencies	Committed
Leadership	Self-managed

Example 7

Values	Traits
Challenge	Self-directed
Trust	Strong work ethic
Sense of purpose	Conscientious
Personal development	Systematic
Clear communication	Persistent

Example 8

Values	Traits
Relationships	Intrapreneurial
Inclusivity	Diplomatic
Ethical leadership	Empowering
Progress	Imaginative
Meaning	Challenger

Evaluating organizations' values and traits

I am often asked how one can know if the values an organization lists on their website truly represent how they run the company. This is when you have to do your due diligence. We can't rely on what organizations put up on their websites. This content is usually written by sales and marketing teams – greenwashing is a real phenomenon, unfortunately! – and is not enough on its own to tell you much about the organization's inner culture.

Ideally, we want to get insider intel from a human being. Try to find people who work there now or have recently left (the latter may be more truthful), and talk to them about their experience with the organization. This will help you to discover what authentic and practical values are at play there.

Many organizations provide directories of their staff and boards on their websites. Try seeking out people in roles that might interact with the one that interests you, and then do an internet search for those people to see if you can unearth contact information for them. One trick that sometimes works is to search for their name in combination with the company URL extension. So if you were trying to find Stella Andrews at Acme Widgets, and the organization website is www.acmewidgets. com, then you would search for 'Stella Andrews "@acmewidgets.com"'. Other places that often feature names and contact information include:

- organizational PowerPoint presentations;
- conference programmes;
- legally mandated reporting (for publicly traded companies, this is on the investor relations section of the website);
- press releases (most larger organizations have a media portal on their website).

Don't overlook the simple value of picking up the phone. It can't hurt to call the main number and see if you can get through to someone. If you encounter an unhelpful human on your first attempt, try calling out of hours to see if you get an automated directory. These can often put you straight through to the right person. In Step 11, we will cover how to use LinkedIn to help you reach a real person, and we'll get into the ins and outs of networking in Step 13.

Basically, you need to show your ability to source and build relationships, as the impact sector is all based on stakeholder relations and influencing. It's important to show some ingenuity in your job hunt by reaching out to friends of friends (second-level connections on LinkedIn, for example), by picking up the phone, by doing something to connect with a live person, not hiding behind email. If you can't demonstrate this ability, a recruiter or hiring manager may well have a hard time believing that you have the skills to build key relationships and partnerships in your dream purpose-driven role.

Case Study   Christina Forst

Christina transitioned from more than six years in in-house roles at multinational financier and insurer AIG into a sustainability management consulting role at Context America. Thinking back on her process, Christina says, 'It's not always easy to define the things you value or the type of worker you are, but the values and traits exercise helped me start to build my personal brand story around keywords that I wanted to be known for, while also making sure that my next role matched my values as well.' (Walk of Life, 2020)

KEY POINTS

In this chapter, we looked at the importance of:

- defining our own values and traits;
- evaluating the values and traits of the organizations that appeal to us.

What's next?

Now that we've drilled down on your defining values and traits, we'll turn in Step 5 to unpacking some of the fears you have about making a career change. If you need to go back to your values and traits lists and refine them, this is a great time to do so. We'll be using them again as we move through the steps.

References and further reading

Stanford Report (2005) [accessed 15 November 2019] *'You've got to find what you love', Jobs says*. 12 June [Online] https://news.stanford.edu/news/2005/june15/jobs-061505.html (archived at https://perma.cc/WDH5-8YRD)

Walk of Life [accessed 14 September 2020] *Client Stories – Christina Forst* [Online] https://walkoflifecoaching.com/client-stories/christina-forst/ (archived at https://perma.cc/DBU7-PY22)

Change your course

How do I overcome my fears and enhance my impact credentials?

We've got a pretty good sense of the impact market landscape, and spent some time determining how you might best fit within it. In the process, you may have identified a gap in your skills. People can feel a bit confused or daunted as to how to augment their impact credentials. In my experience, jobseekers at this stage often fall into a few key traps:

- taking a pay cut;
- taking a lower-level job;
- keeping options too broad/open;
- going back to school;
- getting a sustainability certification they don't really need; or
- scrolling the internet aimlessly for impact jobs.

In this step, we'll cover how to avoid these traps. Before we get to that, though, we'll first discuss some of the barriers around making a career change, chief among which is fear. We'll also look at how to gain experience and build skills for the purpose economy, including through strategic volunteering, fellowships and competitions. Finally, we'll talk about how to create and pitch your own impact role.

Why this step is important

Jobseekers respond in all sorts of ways to shortfalls in their experience... and some ways are a whole lot more helpful than others. Typically, the worst responses are born of fear, so we're going to spend some time in this step thinking about fear, and how to manage it so that it doesn't undermine your job search. We'll then discuss some practical, actionable tips for closing any gaps you may have in your résumé.

Making a career change

What scares you about a career change? There are a million reasons *not* to look for a new job, even if you're unhappy in your current role. Job searching is a lot of work! You have to figure out how your skills will translate, what the market is like now, and how you'll find the time for a job search while balancing all of your life's existing demands. However, with the right approach, making a career change can be as exhilarating as it is scary. Fears of change, failure and the unknown are usually what hold us back from making the leap. Rather than resisting your fears, use them to their best advantage by recognizing them and putting them to work.

EXERCISE   The next three years

Imagine yourself three years forward in your job or career.

- Did you have an impact in those three years?
- Did you make a difference?
- Did you challenge yourself to grow?
- Did you enable others to live into their values?

What do those three years need to look like for you to meet your personal and professional goals?

Fear of change

As humans, we have evolved a 'fight or flight' response to potential dangers. It's what helped our hominid ancestors decide whether to do battle with predators, or to flee quick-sharp up a tree. Once the situation that gave rise to the fear is over, the body reverts to its non-stress state.

Today, however, we're bombarded with choices and have to think on our feet; what's more, we apply fear to future situations that haven't even yet arisen. Moving beyond fear requires an acknowledgement that fear is an irrational reaction in most contexts – we're no longer being chased up trees by sabre-toothed tigers – and that rather than being afraid, it's far more productive to examine our reactions in order to move past them responsibly. Mindfulness helps.

When it comes to making a career change, how people feel about it is always a very personal thing, but some of the most common concerns I hear are:

- The impact market is highly competitive.
- The 'easy' route of finding a role online is now far less likely to convert to a job than networking, which for many is not a comfortable sport.

- They have to confidently create and communicate their personal impact brand to stand out from the crowd, which many people find distasteful because it feels like bragging. Others struggle with impostor syndrome, questioning their ability to excel in their dream sustainability role.
- Sustainability is an evolving and diverse agenda that differs in each company and each sector, so navigating the jobs market around it is not clear or straightforward.
- A change could lead to a loss of status or security.
- They might try and try again and still fail.
- The impact space is relatively unknown to them, and they might regret their decision to move into it and wish they had taken the easy route.

Do any of these ring true for you? You can overcome your own fears by first clarifying them, naming them, and writing them down. Then you can study them in the cold light of day, and ask why they're holding you back. At the same time, though, remember that fear is often intuition in disguise. By extracting the useful warning your intuition has identified, you can make fear work for you. Once you've created your mapping, look at your fears and ask yourself the following questions:

- Is this fear valid? Is the story in your head true? Is it something I can control? Is it about me and my abilities, or the external environment?
- What is the worst-case scenario that could arise from this fear?
  - What factors would make this outcome more likely?
  - How can I minimize each of those factors?
- What is the best-case scenario that could arise from this fear?
  - What factors would make this outcome more likely?
  - How can I maximize each of those factors?

By shining a spotlight on your fears, you make them manageable and reduce their power over you.

EXERCISE   Mapping your fears

Think about what's really holding you back from making your dream career change into the purpose economy. The career change fear map in Table 5.1 provides some examples of common fears. Fill in the subsequent blank rows with your own. Start by listing your top five fears. In the second column, write down an action you can take to overcome each fear. This should be a real-time action you can take in the coming weeks – something specific and tangible. In the last column, write down the people or resources that can help you to achieve your action and overcome your fear.

TABLE 5.1   Career change fear map

Fear holding you back	Action you can take to overcome it... now	Who/what can help you?
Time to find new roles	Set aside 1 hour, twice a week for research	My husband can take the kids at that time
Perceived gap in skillset	Identify which skills are required and translate yours to be relevant	Career coach
Hate networking	Write an elevator pitch and three things you can offer to your network	*How to Become a Key Person of Influence* book by Daniel Priestley (2014)
1		
2		

TABLE 5.1 *continued*

Fear holding you back	Action you can take to overcome it... now	Who/what can help you?
3		
4		
5		

Tips for making a career change for impact

Let's work through some practical, actionable tips for making a career change into your dream impact role.

1. You can change – just not everything all at once

As we covered in Step 3 with our Impact Onion exercise, the best strategy is to change one layer at a time. You may need to take an interim step in order to complete the big change you want to make in another year or two.

2. Taking a step back in your career doesn't help your chances

My clients often tell me they're willing to take a pay cut and start at the bottom. This is almost always a mistake: never undervalue yourself. It tells your audience you think you aren't good enough, and they'll believe it. Overqualification is also a legitimate concern on the part of employers. If you were the hiring manager, would you want to manage someone with an MBA and seven years' experience if you were just looking for a bachelor's degree plus three years? The idea of supervising a bored, underused employee holds little appeal. The problem can quickly compound itself in your job search, too. Imagine how demotivated and deflated you'd feel if you didn't even get called for roles you could do in your sleep.

Aim for roles that are at your level and show career progression, so you look confident about the value you bring to the table.

3. Going back to school doesn't buy you a job

Based on the work you did in Steps 1 and 2, you should know what education and certifications other professionals in your target role have. A few common certifications in the impact space include:

- Leadership in Energy and Environmental Design (LEED);
- Certified Sustainability Assurance Practitioner (CSAP);
- Global Reporting Initiative (GRI) Certified Training Partner;
- Certified Sustainable Development Professional (CSDP).

However: don't be fooled into thinking that a degree or a school's career centre will get you a job after you graduate. A master's degree is a huge investment, both in time and money. If you pursue a full-time programme, you also incur the opportunity cost of not working. Not only that, but practical, tangible work experience is worth its weight in gold in the sustainability space.

That being said, graduate school is an excellent place to gain professional connections and expand your network, focus on subject-specific knowledge, and add additional credentials to your CV. If you are considering the international development field, a master's degree is becoming increasingly necessary to advance in that particular space.

Graduate school also provides opportunities to pursue fellowships and enter competitions that can help you to build your personal impact brand. Some of the fellowships in the impact space are offered by:

- Acumen;
- Echoing Green;
- Environmental Defense Fund (EDF);
- National Resources Defense Council (NRDC);
- RSF Social Finance.

The following organizations sponsor competitions that centre on sustainability:

- Ashoka Changemakers;
- Climate CoLab;
- Global Social Venture Competition (GSVC);
- Kellogg-Morgan Stanley Sustainable Investing Challenge;
- NRG-COSIA Carbon XPRIZE.

If you do decide to get further training, make sure that you truly need it, and that it is part of the requirements for your dream job. Keep in mind, there are many certifications available to improve your skills and knowledge that take a lot less time and money than a formal master's degree.

If you elect to pursue a master's and the programme includes a master's project, make sure to position that on your CV as real work experience as an MBA or Master's Consultant. Be explicit that it was part of a degree programme, and make sure not to imply that you were a full-time employee of the organization.

TECHNICAL SKILLS IN THE PURPOSE ECONOMY

If you're technically minded, there are several skillsets that are in increasingly high demand in the impact sector. Artificial intelligence (AI), machine learning and sophisticated data analysis are playing a growing role in this space:

- Electric utilities are using AI to analyse data coming from smart meters on customers' properties to evaluate opportunities for energy efficiency.

- Environmental NGOs are using drones to measure and tabulate methane emissions at oil and gas wellheads. They're attributing those emissions to individual companies, and then comparing their findings with those companies' disclosures to see if they line up. And they're using machine learning to model likely future emissions under companies' reported growth strategies.

- Research providers who advise investors on the sustainability attributes of their portfolios are using AI and machine learning to mine novel sources of insight into companies and compare their findings against what those companies say about their social and environmental performance. For example, AI is being used to crawl through social media posts by employees and conduct something called 'sentiment analysis' to evaluate the health of a company's relationship with its employees.

AI appears poised to shift the needle around the sustainability agenda, and I expect that in 20 years, we're going to look back and say it was a game changer.

Another important technical area in the impact sector is life cycle analysis (LCA), which is a method used to evaluate the environmental impact of a product through all the stages of its life cycle: extraction and processing of the raw materials, manufacturing, distribution, use, recycling and final disposal. A growing number of universities, including Columbia and Temple, have departments and degree programmes dedicated to LCA training.

Blockchain is a relatively young technology that has significant applications in the impact space. Blockchain is essentially a digital ledger technology, where bits of information are added at each step in a process to create a digital trail. It's being used to support visibility and tracing in global supply chains, to track information related to human and labour rights, forest and fisheries stewardship, and other topics of concern in the purpose economy. Skills required from blockchain professionals include web development and cryptography. Numerous entities offer blockchain certification training.

4. Helping an NGO can help your chances

I've heard from numerous hiring managers in the purpose economy who say they've hired candidates because of their volunteer work experience. In the sustainability arena, volunteering can help to prove your commitment to the issue areas on which you want to work. Strategic volunteering uses your core skills, allows you to achieve tangible results, and plugs you into additional networks that can support your job search.

If you pursue strategic volunteer work, make sure to take on high-quality projects with tangible, skills-based results that contribute to your overall proposition. Set yourself simple key performance indicators (KPIs) that you can work toward, like 'helped X unemployed 18-year-olds open a bank account' if you work in the financial sector. Pick a charity organization whose mission is aligned with your interests, one you'd like to work with for three to five years. Outputs and impacts don't happen overnight, and you'll want to demonstrate that you can be relied upon to see your commitments through.

Make sure to connect with everyone in your volunteer space, both professionals and other volunteers, on LinkedIn and other social media. This helps to deepen and diversify your network of contacts. Make sure the volunteer role you have taken on offers you access to stakeholders in the sector in which you ultimately want to work.

There are several resources available in the purpose economy to help you volunteer strategically:

- The **Taproot Foundation** is a great place to start. They aim to align hard business skills and experience (yours) with organizations committed to solving social and environmental problems. Check out their database of pro bono projects and get inspired.
- Another option for finance professionals is **Bankers Without Borders**. This unique organization has tasked itself with

partnering Fortune 500 companies and individuals with organizations fighting global poverty to improve their scale, sustainability, and impact.

- **Ashoka** is the largest global network of social entrepreneurs and offers many opportunities. Among my favourites are the chief entrepreneur and leadership listings aimed specifically at experienced entrepreneurs and intrapreneurs. Ashoka's LinkedIn volunteering group is also quite useful.

If you do pursue strategic volunteering, make sure to professionalize it on your résumé so that it's in the same format as your work experience. You can also create a section called 'Pro Bono Leadership' on your CV. Consider the following examples from some of my clients' résumés:

- **Global Summit of Women**, Washington, DC and Brazil
  Adviser to CEO on 25th anniversary summit in Brazil building a TED piece into high-profile event with President of Brazil, President of Boeing.
- **East Meets West Foundation**, Oakland, CA
  Board Member, Social Enterprise Sub-Committee for international development agency serving disadvantaged people in Asia with programmes in clean water, sanitation and healthcare.
- **10,000 Women**, Lima, Peru
  Adviser alongside microfinance organization, **MiBanco**, to women entrepreneurs on business skills and microfinance opportunities.

We'll dive into the ins and outs of writing a killer CV in Step 8.

5. Calling everyone you know has never been more important

An effective job hunt is about relationships, not about job boards. Fortunately, in the purpose economy, this is a lot more pleasant than in the broader jobs market. Think of it as making new friends, or at least connecting with people who share your passions and interests. If you're dedicated to reducing greenhouse gas emissions in agriculture, chances are that you'll enjoy meeting and interacting with others in that space. Is your mission to improve rural access to safe drinking water and hygiene around the world? That's a pretty great foundation on which to build a relationship with other committed people.

In Step 13, we'll work through the finer points of networking so you can get out there with confidence.

6. Sell your achievements, not your responsibilities

It's far more compelling to tell your story in terms of your accomplishments, rather than your duties. Say what you delivered, why you were proud of it, and what was in it for your employer. That's what will make you stand out among hundreds of other job applicants.

We'll work through this in detail in Step 8. Now, let's tackle the one-page job proposal.

Creating your own role

In today's competitive impact jobs market, we have to get creative. Sometimes, we might even need to create a job for ourselves. A job proposal, much like a business proposal, shows a potential employer what you can offer and why it will benefit them to have a conversation with you, and hopefully to hire you. With your proposal, you're effectively saying, 'This is what I can do for you.'

Writing a one-page impact job proposal

The one-page impact job proposal looks to the future instead of recording the past. Where a cover letter aims to land the jobseeker a specific role in a specific industry with a specific organization, a job proposal seeks to solve a problem at a given organization and create value in a new role, with room for that role to evolve over time.

It's best to use a one-page impact job proposal when:

- you're seeking buy-in for a new project;
- you've found an organization you want to work for, but there's no opening;
- there's an opening, but not at the right level, so you want to see if you can do something else for them;
- you have an internal contact who's willing to put you forward, but there's no direct fit for you at the moment; or
- you want to go freelance and pitch yourself in for project work.

When writing a one-page impact job proposal, follow this three-step formula:

1. *Pitch to their challenge.* Consider the pain points you're trying to solve for the organization you're targeting.
2. *Pitch what you do.* What specifically will you do to ease their pain?
3. *Pitch your summary story.* How can you grab their attention in a few key sentences?

1. PITCH TO THEIR CHALLENGE

Let's look at those steps a little more closely, using the example of a media/online communications role for an alternative food company.

First, start with a title and subtitle that label and define the entire proposal:

Job Proposal for Online Media Role in Brooklyn

Next, we need to pitch to the organization's challenge. Remember, this is the first paragraph in your pitch, and it needs to grab the decision-maker's attention – in this example, it is likely to be the organization's sustainability director. In order to effectively grab their attention, you will need to do your research. Once you've identified the companies you want to target, go on their websites and read everything you can about their sustainability initiatives. Look closely at their sustainability reports. What are their key targets for the next phase of implementation? In which areas are they weak? Then look at their competitors. What are they doing? What are their sectoral benchmarks?

Using the information you're able to gather, imagine you already have a job in their team and devise a solution for them that you're uniquely positioned to deliver. Break this down into a concise, compelling paragraph – try to use the company's own language and data as much as possible. Make it clear that you know what they're trying to achieve, you have a solution, and you have a plan to deliver it.

Here's our example:

Alternative food organizations like <name of company> need a fresh voice across diverse platforms to gain presence alongside conventional food messaging. From <name of company>'s mission and activities, one of your challenges may be to engage the next generation of eaters with a source of fresh, well-made, nourishing foods that will best meet their individual nutritional, taste and budgetary needs.

2. PITCH WHAT YOU DO

Follow with four or five lines that set out what you do – your who, what, why and how, and your concise goal.

- Your 'who' is what you want the reader to remember about you.
- Your 'what' is the sustainability value you can bring to their team.
- Your 'why' is the unique benefit you can bring to their impact efforts.
- Your 'how' describes what distinguishes you from the competition.

- Your goal establishes your immediate objectives and what you expect the reader to do for you, and vice versa.

Think of this section as an elevator pitch: a brief, persuasive synopsis of an idea that you can deliver in the time it takes to complete a short elevator ride. This becomes a valuable verbal networking tool for you to use at conferences and meetings as well, when someone asks the dreaded question, 'So what do you do?'

Here's our example:

In order to achieve this, sustainable food retailers need to make positive messages speak louder to consumers than their default of cheap, convenient, processed foods. I would welcome the opportunity to contribute to this goal by helping you to scale up the creation of engaging online content to support the next stage of growth. I combine seven years of lean grassroots content creation, marketing and community building where I have advised founders of small businesses and published thought leadership on food, nutrition and environmental policy.

You want to influence the growing conversation around health, nutrition and sustainability in the food system, and to support both consumers and suppliers in their journey towards wellbeing. This is also my calling. With my combined communications and nutrition background, I could help <name of company> expand its reach to new and dynamic audiences, specifically by using digital media for e-commerce. By synthesizing seasonal trends, recipe ideas, cooking tips, and food movement activity, I would support your content and marketing efforts in both strategy development and implementation.

3. PITCH YOUR SUMMARY STORY

Last, pitch your summary story. You only have one chance to make a first impression, and the final paragraph of your pitch needs to convey a strong sense of the authentic you. This is where your personal profile comes in, to communicate why this organization should work with you and how you fit into their culture. This part shouldn't be longer than four or five sentences, and should include:

1 your descriptive title, the years of professional experience you have, and what your overall impact has been to date;
2 your top skills and sectors;
3 what sets you apart, such as languages, education, or overseas experience; and
4 your objective, a reiteration of your first paragraph that shows how you will help them, not the other way around.

From our example:

My passion for good food, healthy communities, non-traditional media and start-ups is proven through my professional work, as well as my personal adventures. While preparing my master's thesis, titled 'Increasing Consumer Involvement with Sustainable Foods through Health Promotion', I first explored the links between health, food behaviour, and environmentally sustainable outcomes. In addition, I've simultaneously used my personal food blog (TheHomeGrownTomato.com (archived at https://perma.cc/ E6M9-8NSY)) and careers podcast (Good on Paper) to maximize impact using different content delivery methods.

As a communications and marketing manager with seven years' experience growing sustainability-focused organizations, I have used brand voices to generate positive social impact while meeting bottom-line targets. I have diverse skills in building day-to-day processes and translating big vision into tangible initiatives for small businesses and start-ups in the environmental, food and health sectors.

Finally, it's time to bring it home. Keep it short and memorable. Our example concludes with a single line:

I love food. Let's talk.

Once you've got your pitch together, find the physical and/or email addresses and names of the relevant directors at your target organization. Try to follow up your one-page pitch email with a phone call if you can, to give it the human touch. Including graphics or a video always gets people's attention.

While many people can find this process uncomfortably close to bragging, it's more a matter of compelling storytelling. The person in our example presents an enticing idea, and focuses on the organization instead of themselves – it's hard not to want to meet them to learn more. We have to self-promote in this process, but if we do it according to our personal style with confidence and clarity, it stands a good chance of landing well and piquing the reader's interest.

Case Study   Rochelle March

Rochelle spent years providing strategic advice on increasing efficiencies and maximizing opportunities for innovation to clients in a variety of sectors, before moving to a full-time strategy role with SustainAbility. Reflecting on our work together, Rochelle says, 'The Career Change Fear Map helped me to identify my blocks so that I could break them down and start to chip away at them through using the other tools like translating my skills for my new audience. Without this, I probably wouldn't have made the change as quickly.'

> **KEY POINTS**
>
> In this chapter, we looked at how to:
>
> - overcome the fear of career change;
> - make a career change for impact; and
> - create our own impact role.

What's next?

Now that we've worked through our fears and barriers associated with a career change toward the purpose economy, we'll move on to designing and writing a compelling brand story and cover the necessary steps to nailing the job application process.

References and further reading

Bankers Without Borders [accessed 8 September 2020] About Us [Online] https://www.bankerswithoutborders.com/about (archived at https://perma.cc/3K94-4US6)

Hoggard, E (2017) [accessed 8 September 2020] *Recognize Your Fight or Flight (or Freeze) Responses*, happiful [Online] https://happiful.com/recognise-your-fight-or-flight-or-freeze-responses/ (archived at https://perma.cc/299Q-YX92)

Houde, S (2014) [accessed 8 September 2020] *Dear Shannon, How Can I Face My Fear of Making a Career Change?*, Greenbiz [Online] https://www.greenbiz.com/article/dear-shannon-how-can-i-face-my-fear-making-career-change (archived at https://perma.cc/Q496-J8K8)

Houde, S (2014) [accessed 8 September 2020] *Why a One-Page Job Proposal Is Worth Way More Than a CV*, Greenbiz [Online] https://www.greenbiz.com/article/why-one-page-job-proposal-worth-way-more-cv (archived at https://perma.cc/FXF3-KJAH)

Houde, S [accessed 8 September 2020] *Here's How a Master's Degree and Strategic Volunteering Can Help Move Your Impact Career Forward*, Walk of Life Coaching [Online] https://walkoflifecoaching.com/heres-how-a-masters-degree-and-strategic-volunteer-can-help-move-your-impact-career-forward/ (archived at https://perma.cc/EPW6-A9GM)

Priestley, D (2014) *Key Person of Influence: The five-step method to become one of the most highly valued and highly paid people in your industry* (revised edition), Rethink Press, London

PART THREE

Map your story

Be in their shoes

How do I unpack what the hiring manager really wants when I don't know the lingo?

Now that you've worked on overcoming your fears, it's time to make some tangible preparations for your impact job search.

We all know how it feels to have our heart jump at the thought of finding our dream job online, and that feeling of urgency to customize our cover letters and résumés and get them out the door. Not so fast! If we want to see real success, it's important to be methodical in preparing for the job application process.

Why this step is important

Hiring managers will only spend six seconds reading a résumé for the first time, so it's critical to tick their boxes clearly, right off the bat (Jackson, 2017). This step outlines the key tasks to complete when applying for an impact role, as well as the importance of doing a 45-minute job description rewrite before beginning the application. This exercise provides a solid understanding of the skills and language the hiring manager is looking to match, so that you can use that same language in your application to resonate with the hiring manager and distinguish yourself from the competition.

The job application process

If a job application doesn't meet the hiring manager's requirements, it's probably going straight in the bin. So how can you be sure yours doesn't suffer that fate?

If you follow this guide to doing job applications, you'll greatly increase your chances of getting an interview call.

Task 1: Do LinkedIn research on anyone and everyone you know at the organization, including 1st and 2nd connections.

Task 2: Extract keywords and themes from those people's profiles so you can align the language you use in your CV and online profile to be relevant and resonant with the space you're targeting.

Task 3: Follow the organization on LinkedIn.

Task 4: Reach out to any 1st connection contacts at the organization by phone to get intel on the role:

- Where are they in the recruitment process? It's often the case that jobs are still posted even though the hiring manager is in final rounds of interviews, so this will save you time on applying if they already have someone.
- Why is the role open? Is it a new role, or did someone leave? This can give you some insight into the company culture.

Task 5: If you don't have any 1st connections at the organization, contact the people you have in common with your 2nd connections and write a blurb for them to forward on your behalf to introduce you. Don't panic if you don't have any 2nd connections, either. We'll talk more about LinkedIn in Step 11 and general networking in Step 13, but the basic message here is that you have to work the system. Connect with anyone and everyone you know, and make it part of your job to nurture and maintain that network. It is a vital tool in the jobseeker's tool belt, especially in the impact space.

Task 6: Complete the job description rewrite tool, which we're about to do later in this step.

Task 7: Customize a maximum of 20 per cent of your template CV (Step 8) and cover letter (Step 9) to match keywords and themes from your job description rewrite.

Task 8: Have a friend, family member, or other third party do final edits for formatting against the CV checklist tool that we'll work on in Step 8.

TIP   Job application pointers

- Contact one person a day from your network.
- Have one live coffee – or video call, if you're remote – per week.
- Only apply to roles where your skills mapping from Step 3 proves you could beat out 190 other applicants.
- Formal applications should take four to six hours to complete.

The job description rewrite

Now let's drill down on Task 6 of the job application process, where we rewrite a job description so that you can analyse more deeply exactly what the hiring manager is looking for. This is actually the most important task in the job application process.

In all my years of recruiting, I have never seen a decently written job description that makes it easy for a candidate to match what they are selling to what is required. This is often because job descriptions are written by someone in human resources who may not understand the role as well as the people who perform the functions in question. Or the description may be a company template with a few key requirements that are edited for each role. The result is an unnecessarily long document that candidates tend to skim, rather than dissecting it for its critical elements. But we can fix this.

Instead of skimming a job description and saying to yourself, 'I can do that, I can also do that, well ... I have done something similar to that...' and then jumping into your CV and cover letter without really testing if you can prove it all, first spend 45 minutes on our job description rewrite tool.

DON'T CONFUSE CV ELEMENTS!

The job description rewrite process allows us to unpack and recategorize (usually poorly written) job description details into our key Impact Onion areas from Step 3 – values, traits, skills and impact issues.

It's important not to confuse sector and industry with impact issues, and not to confuse knowledge and expertise with skills.

Mixing these together only muddies a jobseeker's narrative and makes it more difficult to understand what they offer.

An example may help to illustrate this point. I reviewed a CV that listed climate expertise as a skill. But it isn't. It's an impact issue, which we sometimes call 'issue expertise' or 'issue management' in the impact space. Climate expertise sits as an umbrella over all of the skills and tasks one would perform in a climate-focused role. A person may do strategy, policy, monitoring, and reporting all about climate, but climate itself is not a skill.

This person also had done this work for 15 years in the energy industry. They needed to deconstruct the job description for the role they were pursuing to see where their industry knowledge (not skill) might be most relevant and useful to a new, modern

---

> audience. The job description rewrite tool allows us to tease out what the hiring manager is really asking for, and build it back up into a clearer, more compelling story.

This is quite a meaty assignment, so make sure to give yourself enough time to work through it. This will save you time later, I promise.

This exercise is designed to help you gain clarity about what skills are required for your target industry/roles and to identify how your proven skills match those requirements. We'll work on an example first, and then you can do one of your own.

Job description rewrite

Task 1: Read the job specifications and decide on the four skill categories that most of their requirements would fit into. Include all text from top to bottom, whether in the description, the responsibilities, or the requirements sections.

Task 2: Cut and paste all key phrases (eliminate all extra words) from the job description into a new document and place them under the four skills categories.

Task 3: Highlight all keywords in the new document to make sure you will be key-word searchable in LinkedIn and human resources databases.

Recruiters do keyword searches on LinkedIn, and all have their own databases of candidates. A second audience would be in-house recruiters in a company who would be doing the same thing. Example: If you're looking for a job in sustainable agriculture, use language like small-holder farmers, sustainable supply chain, cacao, coffee.

Task 4: Print this document and have it next to you as you design your master CV based on these requirements.

Let's work through an example first so you can see how this looks in practice.

EXAMPLE JOB DESCRIPTION

3P Consulting: People, Planet, Profit
Senior consultant
Job context
Welcome to 3P Consulting. For more than 10 years we have been a leading provider of sustainability consulting services for Fortune 500 and FTSE250 companies across all sectors. With our clients, we advise on how to catalyse progress on social and environmental sustainability across their complex supply chains. Using the frameworks of design thinking and systems thinking, we encourage them to push beyond their comfort zones of addressing operational, reputational and regulatory risks, and to convert these into innovative opportunities to lead in their sector.

We are seeking to recruit a highly motivated and collaborative Senior Consultant to join our US team.

Accountability
You will report to the Director of Consulting Services.

Job summary and mission
This 3P Senior Consultant role is responsible for client relations, project management and strategy design. The Senior Consultant will also contribute to the collaborative thought leadership and brand development. You will engage with your internal team to deliver on projects as well as with external contractors and suppliers as needed. Your mission is to enable our clients to push forward in their own ambition of stretching beyond the SDG targets and a net zero world. You will lead the delivery of high-quality consulting services for our clients, with a focus on advancing sustainability decisions, management and communication founded in science and market insights.

Responsibilities

- Perform various types of sustainability consulting services, including:
    - strategic analysis; materiality assessments; benchmarking; research into client sustainability issues; support

development of company and product sustainability strategies; sustainability communications, etc;

- ○ lead or participate in (depending on level of technical analysis skills) impact assessment projects such as science-based targets, company or product carbon footprints, etc.
- Prepare interim and final client deliverables.
- Lead client interactions, such as project meetings/calls, etc.
- Maintain and enhance client relationships and identify opportunities for additional project work with clients.
- Drive communication of 3P's thought leadership to clients.
- Manage a targeted number of internal projects, based on interests, experience, skills and 3P's needs.
- Keep up to date with market trends and industry regulations in sustainability, social impact and the environment to inform ongoing development of 3P's services.
- Shape new and innovative products, services, frameworks, white papers and tools to advance 3P's competitiveness.

Required skills

- ability to analyse, understand and communicate technical sustainability topics – both qualitative and quantitative;
- client relationship development; new business development; understanding and anticipating client needs; seeing and communicating implications and bigger picture;
- ability to translate complex information into clear, compelling insights and recommendations;
- strong written and verbal communication skills (results presentations, pitches/offers, slide decks, public speaking);
- strategy; benchmarking; SWOT analysis; frameworks; systems thinking;
- deep understanding of sustainability topics, services, market needs relevant to 3P;
- expertise in two to three sustainability issues related to the SDGs;

- anticipate future risks, challenges, opportunities, new solutions/ approaches;
- deep knowledge of two to three industries/sectors including their stakeholders and supply chains.

Character attributes

- combination of analytical strength, intellectual curiosity and excellent interpersonal skills;
- dependable/reliable;
- resilient/persevering in face of research challenges, thorny strategic questions;
- self-motivated to do high-quality work in an efficient manner;
- team-orientated and collaborative;
- intellectual and business curiosity – business models, performance, news.

Qualifications

- master's in sustainability or business;
- 5–10 years' experience in a client-facing role;
- knowledge of the SDGs, Global Reporting Initiative, and LCAs preferred.

To succeed in the 3P culture, candidates must be intrapreneurs and innovative thinkers. We are looking for people who operate as business partners to their clients and internal team mates, aim to deliver excellence, and who listen well in order to be ahead of the market needs. 3P is an Equal Opportunity Employer committed to a diversified and inclusive workforce.

Example job description rewrite

Let's follow the tasks that we covered above to rewrite this job description. For Task 1, identify the four skill categories that most of the requirements fit into. For Task 2, cut and paste all keywords and phrases (deleting all superfluous words) from the job description into a new document, and place them under the four skill categories. Here's how these two tasks would look in our example:

SKILL CATEGORIES

Strategy and market research

- materiality assessments;
- benchmarking;
- SWOT analysis, frameworks, systems thinking;
- research into client sustainability issues;
- develop company and product sustainability strategies;
- market trends and industry regulations;
- innovative products, services, frameworks, white papers and tools;
- anticipate future risks and opportunities;
- new solutions/approaches.

Client relations and business development

- prepare interim and final client deliverables;
- lead client interactions, such as project meetings/calls, etc;
- maintain and enhance client relationships and identify opportunities for additional project work with clients;
- client relationship development; new business development; understanding and anticipating client needs, seeing and communicating implications and bigger picture.

Project management

- Manage a targeted number of internal projects, based on interests, experience, skills and 3P's needs.

Analysis and communications

- drive communication of 3P's thought leadership to clients;

- ability to analyse, understand and communicate technical sustainability topics – both qualitative and quantitative;
- ability to translate complex information into clear, compelling insights and recommendations;
- strong written and verbal communication skills (results presentations, pitches/offers, slide decks, public speaking);
- deep understanding of sustainability topics, services, market needs relevant to 3P.

In Task 3, we want to capture and highlight all keywords from the job specifications. Understanding your audience's language is crucial to being relevant to them.

There will be language and requirements that don't fit neatly into skill categories, which we can map into other categories like sector, education, values and traits. It's helpful to pull these apart – most job listings mix them together, which can lead a jobseeker to miss a key skill or confuse a trait for a skill.

Make sure to tease out and match terminology like sustainability, corporate responsibility, systems thinking, sustainable business, and so on. Every job listing will reference these a bit differently, as organizations are not consistent in how they discuss the impact agenda.

Here's how Task 3 would look in our example:

Sector/industry/company

- expertise in two to three sustainability issues related to the SDGs;
- deep knowledge of two to three industries/sectors including their stakeholders and supply chains;
- 5–10 years' experience in a client-facing role;
- knowledge of the SDGs, Global Reporting Initiative and LCAs preferred.

Impact issues knowledge

- knowledge of the SDGs, Global Reporting Initiative and LCAs preferred;
- systems and design thinking;
- net zero targets;
- science.

Values

- intellectual curiosity;
- high-quality work;
- efficiency;
- team collaboration;
- progress;
- innovation.

Traits

- analytical strength;
- interpersonal skills;
- dependable/reliable;
- resilient/persevering;
- self-motivated.

Now that you've seen an example of the job description rewrite, take 45 minutes to work through one on your own.

No job description? That's okay too – you may not have found a specific job opening online. This tool can still be used to help you to make sense of what the market is looking for, and to frame your keywords. Short of having a job description in your hands, you can profile 10 people on LinkedIn to whose positions you aspire. That way you have an idea of the skills and language they are using about their role and their company.

If you really want to get results in your job search, you will do this job description rewrite for every single position you apply for. It's part of a two-phase process: first you do the rewrite, then

you customize your template CV and cover letter to align with
that rewrite.

TIP   The 20 per cent rule

This process is about being honest with yourself. If, after
completing the full job description rewrite, you conclude that you'll
need to customize more than 20 per cent of your CV and cover
letter (which we'll work on in Steps 8 and 9) to meet the
requirements of the job you're targeting, then the role may be too
much of a stretch. You probably won't be able to compete against
the hundreds of other applicants for this role, so it's perhaps best
to leave it there and not expend the hours it takes to do a quality
application.

   The job description rewrite will help you to invest your time
wisely in your search for your dream job. If you find that you
consistently need to customize your CV more than 20 per cent to
meet the requirements of the listings you select, I suggest you go
back to the dream job targeting you did in Step 3 to make sure that
you're narrowing your net appropriately.

Case Study   Courtney Bickert

Courtney Bickert reinvented her more than 20-year career in
international development to move into a corporate partnerships role at
the United Nations Foundation. Two and a half years later, she
transitioned again into a new role as vice-president of external relations
at the German Marshall Fund of the United States. After four years in
that role, Courtney struck out on her own to provide customized
consulting and facilitation services using comedy for social impact.

   Reflecting on her job search efforts, Courtney said, 'I had never taken
the time to unpack and dissect a job description before. This tool saved
me so much time and made me able to sell myself for the role much
more clearly. It also helped me NOT to apply to roles I thought I may
have been qualified for at first read but then realized I wasn't. So worth
the 45-minute investment!'

Courtney also emphasized that the dream job targeting exercise from Step 3 was an important step in her career journey. 'I hadn't thought about how to find my ideal job before that. The dream job targeting exercise helped me to focus on what I really wanted in a job, and to refocus my job search and résumé building around that.'

> **KEY POINTS**
>
> In this chapter, we looked at:
>
> - the impact job application process;
> - how to rewrite a job description to get to the heart of what a hiring manager really wants.

What's next?

Now that you've dissected a job description, identified the key themes, and reflected on how your skills match up, you're probably feeling one of two things: (1) satisfied and confident that you have what it takes to go for and potentially win this role or similar impact roles, or (2) slightly nauseated as you peer into the deep ravine that is your sustainability skills gap.

If it's the latter, take heart – at least you know early, and you've constructively identified the areas you need to work on before going for another role like this one. This would be a good time to revisit Step 5 and evaluate your options for closing your skills gap.

If it's the former, it's time to dig out your old CV and move on to the next phase of the application process – rewriting your CV, where all the hard work of mapping your skills will really pay off.

References and further reading

Houde, S [accessed 14 September 2020] *When Writing Your Resume, Don't Miss Your Target*, Walk of Life Coaching [Online] https://walkoflifecoaching.com/when-writing-your-resume-dont-miss-your-target/ (archived at https://perma.cc/M95Y-Y5G7)

Jackson, A (2017) [accessed 26 November 2019] This is exactly what hiring managers & recruiters look for when scanning resumes, *Glassdoor*, 2 August [Online] www.glassdoor.com/blog/scanning-resumes/ (archived at https://perma.cc/K8XA-DSME)

Prove your skills

How do my skills translate for a mission-driven role?

N ow that we've learned how to analyse a job description to get to the heart of what recruiters truly want, and to map our sustainability skills to match job requirements, let's take the next step and work on translating our skills for a dream impact role.

Many jobseekers are unsure how they can apply their current skills to a job in the impact sector. Fortunately, as the impact agenda evolves and becomes increasingly embedded into core business, the competencies required to achieve success have shifted to more commercially-based skills, making it easier to break in from other career paths if jobseekers can prove their transferable skillset. By taking what you've done in the past, reframing it, and translating it into the language the hiring manager speaks, you can present yourself in a way that's relevant to the position and the company. It's a skill in itself!

Why this step is important

Proving your skills is one of the most important tasks you'll take on as a sustainability jobseeker. These are what your audience – the hiring manager – is essentially buying.

In this step, we'll lay out how best to map those skills and tell a compelling career story that will accentuate your prior experience that's relevant to the impact sector. You will learn how to identify your four top skills, which will then become the framework for your CV in Step 8.

What does 'walk me through your CV' really mean?

When interviewers ask you to walk them through your CV, what do they really want to know? They want to know your proven skills that are relevant to what they need you to do in that particular position. They don't want you to walk them through everything you've done from the beginning of time. Skills link directly to the tasks you will be doing or the activities you will be delivering.

Strategy development, influencing cross-functional teams, and measuring and reporting on progress are the top three tasks for sustainability professionals, so you will want to include these skills in your career story. We are also seeing exclusive responsibility for sustainability efforts moving to increasingly higher-ranking positions within organizations (GreenBiz, 2018). So, what are some of the most common activities in the impact sector?

Activities to deliver

Recent studies have revealed what the people with the jobs you want are doing day to day in the impact sector, from manager level right on up to senior vice president. These are the different activities that you will likely be required to deliver, whether you're in an in-house role or have been hired as a consultant. The top five in-house activities for sustainability practitioners are (Acre, Flag, and Carnstone Partners, 2018):

1 **Corporate responsibility/sustainability strategy development and implementation:** benchmarking competitors and/or peers, performing strategic management analyses, and working with key players inside and outside of the organization to design a three- to five-year plan with measurable targets.

2 **Reporting/performance measurement:** measuring the inputs and outputs of delivering on the strategy, including environmental and social data. Reporting covers how material the issues are to the organization so that investors, donors, or funding agencies can understand how the organization is prioritizing and addressing them.

3 **Stakeholder engagement:** mapping priority stakeholders and their crucial issues, and communicating with them to create better understanding and to jointly design 'shared value' initiatives.

4 **Environment:** performing life cycle assessments or environmental impact assessments, which provide the organization with data on how products or services affect the environment through all stages of the value chain. This activity may include designing innovative projects to offset greenhouse gas emissions.

5 **Community investment:** spearheading partnerships with charities or NGOs. This will cover money invested via philanthropic activities and time invested by employees in volunteering programmes, often with a focus on social issues such as affordable housing, employability, financial inclusion, human rights, education, or healthcare.

For consultants, the top five activities are similar, except that auditing/assurance takes the place of community investment. This activity was once on the in-house top five list, but it may have fallen off because strategic philanthropy and partnerships are gaining momentum as the social issues catch up with the environmental ones. Auditing/assurance has died down in-house as companies are seeing less value in the rigorous reporting required for the return on investment.

As you can see, there aren't many technical activities on this list. The only technical one that *is* there – reporting – is probably done by a team, so it won't necessarily be a deal-breaker for a hiring manager.

The major takeaway? These top five activities are primarily commercial. This is good news for career changers, because it means that – with some clever translation – your experience can be easily reframed to prove that you have what it takes to do the job. To illustrate, if you are an accountant and want to break into the impact sector, you could transfer your skills of data analysis and financial reporting to non-financial reporting for corporate responsibility or sustainability reports, because the skills are very similar.

KEY READING FOR ACTIVITIES, SKILLS AND COMPETENCIES

If you are looking to break into the impact sector, add the following publications to your reading list for insight on the market, language and skills required:

- The Institute of Environmental Management and Assessment's (IEMA) Sustainability Skills Map: https://www.iema.net/ sustainability-skills-map (archived at https://perma.cc/RZA4-N5ZF)

- Cambridge Institute for Sustainability Leadership's Behavioural Competency Model for Sustainability Leaders: https://www.cisl. cam.ac.uk/education/graduate-study/master-of-studies-in-sustainability-leadership/pdfs/a-behavioural-competency-model-for-sustainability.pdf/view (archived at https://perma.cc/8XKW-UNM8)

- The Institute of Corporate Responsibility and Sustainability's (ICRS) Competency Framework: https://icrs.info/cpd/competency-framework (archived at https://perma.cc/HCQ6-RYC9)

What are skills and competencies?

A skill is the ability to do something well, expertise resulting either from practice or natural ability. Sometimes skills may be referred to as competencies, and we have competency frameworks such as those listed above that show trends in the skillsets required for the impact work. The top five competencies for in-house jobs are:

1 Engage with stakeholders.
2 Influence and persuade.
3 Plan and develop strategy.
4 Measure and report impact.
5 Manage projects (Acre, Flag, and Carnstone Partners, 2018).

As you can see, they closely resemble the top five activities to deliver. For consultants, this list is virtually the same, except that research and analysis replaces measure and report impact.

Skills for the future

I am often asked how we can make sure our skills remain relevant as the world changes rapidly around us. It's a fair question, as cloud computing, mobile internet and big data are changing the way people work across nearly every economic sector. Robotics, artificial intelligence and automation are already making some jobs obsolete. The nature of work itself will change as geopolitics, consumer ethics, climate change and access to scarce natural resources become increasingly material to corporate, NGO and government strategies.

These technological and socioeconomic contexts present significant staffing challenges for CEOs. Business leaders must take advantage of the productivity and innovation opportunities that automation technologies present, while simultaneously ensuring a smooth workforce transition. The successful jobseekers of the future will be those who anticipate these trends.

In such a dynamic business environment, it goes without saying that the sustainability sector will have to adapt and evolve in tandem. Those of us working in the field need to prepare now to ensure our careers are future-proof. Here are five of the most important skills for the future that sustainability practitioners should take note of now.

COMPLEX PROBLEM-SOLVING

This is probably the most important skill to have on your CV. Designing solutions to meet complex challenges will be the primary activity of the future sustainability professional, even more so than it is now. Problems will occur across multiple business-critical areas, sometimes out of nowhere, and companies will need people who are ready, willing, and able to respond effectively.

Start thinking about how you can hone your problem-solving abilities in your current position, and look for ways to evidence them on your CV for your next role. It's best not to call it 'problem-solving' on your CV, though, as that's a vague term. Use an accomplishment statement to show the reader what you did and how. We'll cover that more in the next step.

CRITICAL THINKING (AND INNOVATION)

This connects to problem-solving, but it's distinct in that it describes the ability to ask the right questions from a variety of different perspectives and to interrogate the options. It also implies a solid understanding of the business landscape, as well as the trends in technology, science and socioeconomics. Bringing that macro-level view down to the micro level of decision-making and picking apart assumptions and biases will add serious value to your offer as a sustainability professional. Again, we'll talk in the next step about how to prove this to the reader with a solid accomplishment statement that shows how you have challenged the status quo and can think innovatively.

CREATIVITY (AND ADAPTABILITY)

This is something no machine can do. Creativity is crucial to telling and selling sustainability stories, both internally and externally, which you need to do if you want to inspire people and have them follow on the journey. The best sustainability professionals take a creative approach to their work and understand its role in translating complex messages for diverse audiences.

But there's more to creativity than storytelling. It's about the way you respond to change, too, and how adaptable you are. With the modern avalanche of new products, new technologies, and new ways of working, sustainability practitioners will need to get more creative in order to benefit from these changes.

NEGOTIATION (AND INFLUENCING)

This one isn't new, but it is more important than ever. How do you expect to broker change if you can't negotiate effectively? The ability to strike difficult compromises with internal and external stakeholders requires a robust rationale and a titanium-strong evidence base, as well as influence. Some people are born with an innate ability to negotiate, and lucky them! For the rest of us, it's something we learn in the heat of the fire. If you have yet to develop this side of your professional practice, look out for a senior mentor whom you can shadow at meetings. Great negotiation skills can really set you apart in the impact jobs market, so commit to enhancing yours.

Skills for purpose and impact

'Soft skills' or interpersonal skills are important in any workplace, but they are especially important in the impact sector, where progress relies so heavily on persuasion, engagement and coalition-building. According to research by LinkedIn, the top five soft skills most in demand are:

1 creativity;
2 persuasion;
3 collaboration;
4 adaptability;
5 emotional intelligence.

(Pate, 2020)

EMOTIONAL INTELLIGENCE (AND EMPATHY)

Emotional intelligence (EQ) has been on the radar of the corporate talent agenda for many years. Just look at all the mindfulness courses and continuing professional development (CPD) modules that major companies like Google are offering their employees. They understand the importance of being able to keep your ego in check and empathize with other people, especially in high-stress situations when solutions seem hard to find.

EQ is also connected to the ability to coordinate with others and manage teams of people, which are essential skills when moving toward a common goal. Evidencing these more subtle qualities on a CV can be tricky, so look for tangible proof points to highlight in your personal achievement statements.

The primary challenge of impact change makers is to convert the non-converted, to persuade people to join them on the journey. Having relationship management, self-awareness, and communication skills – ie EQ – is absolutely essential for almost all impact roles, because it is essential to navigating the human landscape and persuading people to participate in a purpose-driven mission.

Figure 7.1 illustrates the multiple facets of EQ and how they interact.

In a test of 33 important workplace skills, emotional intelligence was found to be the strongest predictor of performance, explaining a full 58 per cent of success in all types of jobs. The study also found that 90 per cent of top performers are also high in emotional intelligence, while just 20 per cent of bottom performers are high in emotional intelligence (Bradberry, 2020).

The role of the chief sustainability officer (CSO)

Whether you are at this level or simply aspire to be in the C-suite someday, you need to know what is required of this strategic role. The CSO at an organization is the holy grail of impact jobs. A great CSO will push the boundaries of existing norms, innovate and think outside the box, engage and empower others to act, understand others' perspectives, make informed decisions, and be resilient enough to make mistakes. As CSO recruiter Rupert Davis says, 'A great CSO or VP of Sustainability is someone who can think like a combination CMO, CFO, early stage entrepreneur, politician, and top strategy consultant, and very specifically understand and apply that to the culture at hand.'

Successful CSOs consistently possess five key skills:

1 *Change leadership:* CSOs create direction or journey out of uncertainty. Be transparent, outward looking, and joined up.
2 *Commercial credibility:* If you're going to change it, you need to understand it and have credibility, honesty, integrity and passion.
3 *People skills:* A good CSO is an influencer, negotiator, diplomat, storyteller and shepherd, and exudes positivity.
4 *Partnership:* CSOs have the ability to build mutual value.
5 *Innovation:* CSOs spot, translate, and respond to trends.

FIGURE 7.1 The EQ matrix

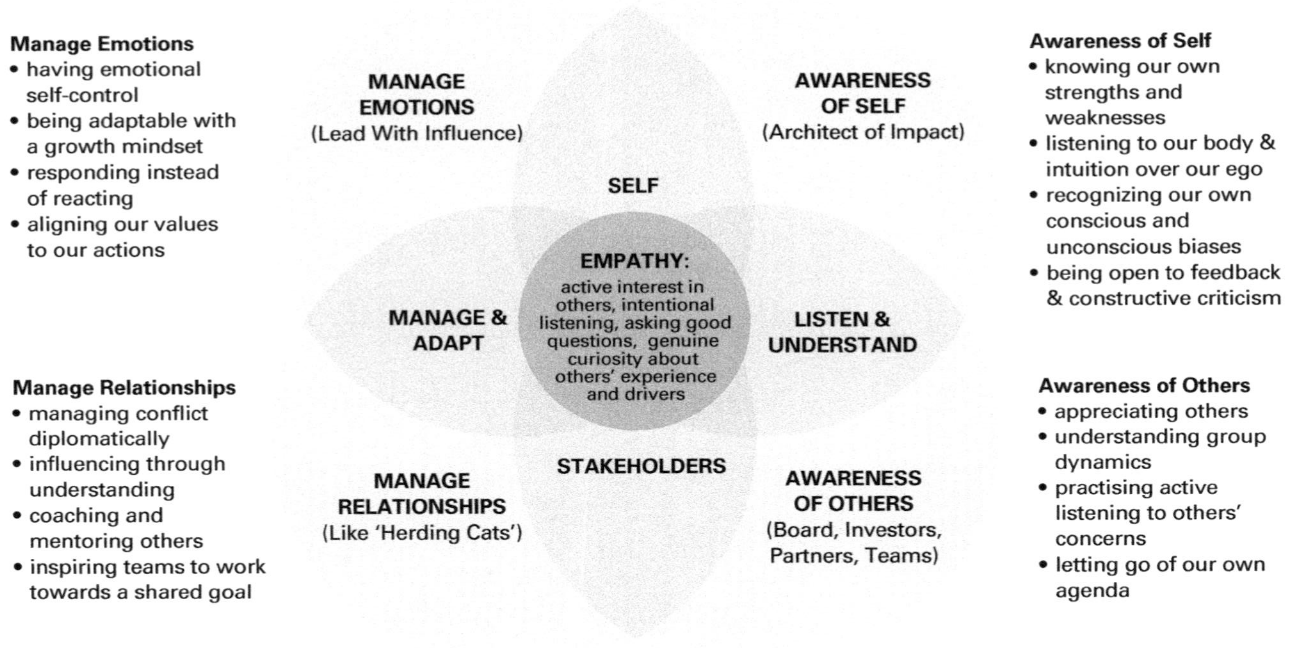

Awareness of Self
- knowing our own strengths and weaknesses
- listening to our body & intuition over our ego
- recognizing our own conscious and unconscious biases
- being open to feedback & constructive criticism

Awareness of Others
- appreciating others
- understanding group dynamics
- practising active listening to others' concerns
- letting go of our own agenda

AWARENESS
OF SELF
(Architect of Impact)

LISTEN &
UNDERSTAND

SELF

EMPATHY:
active interest in others, intentional listening, asking good questions, genuine curiosity about others' experience and drivers

AWARENESS
OF OTHERS
(Board, Investors, Partners, Teams)

STAKEHOLDERS

MANAGE
EMOTIONS
(Lead With Influence)

MANAGE &
ADAPT

MANAGE
RELATIONSHIPS
(Like 'Herding Cats')

Manage Emotions
- having emotional self-control
- being adaptable with a growth mindset
- responding instead of reacting
- aligning our values to our actions

Manage Relationships
- managing conflict diplomatically
- influencing through understanding
- coaching and mentoring others
- inspiring teams to work towards a shared goal

LEADERSHIP IN SUSTAINABILITY

Even if you haven't reached the CSO level, leadership skills are still fundamental to an enduring and successful career in the impact sector. Leadership in sustainability is all about:

- pushing the boundaries of the norms;
- innovating and thinking outside the box;
- engaging and empowering others to act;
- understanding others' perspectives;
- making informed decisions;
- being resilient enough to make mistakes.

What are your skills for success?

In Step 3, we talked about recruiters' fundamental considerations when they evaluate you as a candidate. One of them, of course, is whether or not you can do the job. Naturally, your answer to this question will be an enthusiastic 'Yes, sure I can!' But that won't cut it. You have to prove you have the skills to take on a role in the impact sector by translating your skills and making your experience relevant to the position for which you're applying.

You need to ask yourself three key questions related to tasks or duties:

1 What do you love doing? What goes to the top of your to-do list on a Monday morning?
2 What are you great at? What can you do better than the competition?
3 Does the market need it? Is it relevant to the open position?

The intersection of these three questions is the sweet spot where you want to focus.

Mapping your skills may seem hard at first, but it's so worth it. For many people, it's the most dreaded aspect of the job search. Nevertheless, employers love it, because it makes it easier for them to see readily how what you have done in the past – what you're great at doing – will translate to serve them and their organization today. That's why you'll be glad you did it.

Articulating, positioning and translating your skills for a role or a sector is arguably the most important task you'll undertake as a sustainability jobseeker. The Skills for Success skills mapping tool is designed to do just this. It helps you to do the work for the hiring managers and tell them what you want them to know, rather than telling them everything and hoping they find the relevant threads on their own.

Case Study   Scott Miller

Scott left a career on Wall Street to pursue his passion for promoting environmental and social responsibility. The Skills for Success exercise helped him to develop a simple, four-skill framework to categorize his accomplishments and design a career story that held together around what he could do for the hiring manager. His four skill categories were:

1   business development and strategy;

2   implementation and team;

3   stakeholder engagement;

4   reporting and communications.

Ultimately, Scott reinvented himself as director of business development for the Sustainable Apparel Coalition.

EXERCISE   Map your skills

Now let's define your own top four skill categories, building on what you did in the job description rewrite in Step 6. In the functional CV that we'll be doing together in Step 8, you will see where these four skill categories are going to sit on the first page. They will be your framework for building your 12 accomplishment statements that we'll develop in the next step.

Once you have your top four skill categories written down, define them in more detail using keywords or phrases that you want to make sure you're weaving in, such as in the following example:

- Communications: engage stakeholders, write reports, liaise with press.
- Strategy: design plans, implement policy.
- Project management: deliver on KPIs, manage teams and budgets.
- Research and analysis: qualitative and quantitative, ROI (return on investment), SWOT (strengths, weaknesses, opportunities, threats) analysis.

What are your top four skills, and the keywords or phrases associated with them?

My four skill categories/buckets:

1 _____

2 _____

3 _____

4 _____

Now ask yourself the three key questions we discussed above and record your answers:

1 What do you love doing? What goes to the top of your to-do list on a Monday morning?

2 What are you great at? What can you do better than the competition? What's your unique selling point?

3 What does your target market need? What's relevant to the position that's open, as outlined in the job description and in the competency trends detailed above?

Think of measurable and tangible words, terms, or phrases like 'develop strategy', 'promote buy-in', 'manage projects and teams', 'engage stakeholders', and 'drive bottom line'. Make sure you choose words that are backed up elsewhere in your CV, or you run the risk of derailing your career story.

What is your own sweet spot (see Figure 7.2), paying particular attention to the intersection in the middle? Importantly, these are skills that you not only are *good* at or *like* doing, but that you are *great* at and *love* doing. But the crucial circle of the diagram here asks whether your target audience – the market – needs those skills. This is where passion, talent and marketability come together! You will use it to develop your functional CV in Step 8.

FIGURE 7.2   The sweet spot

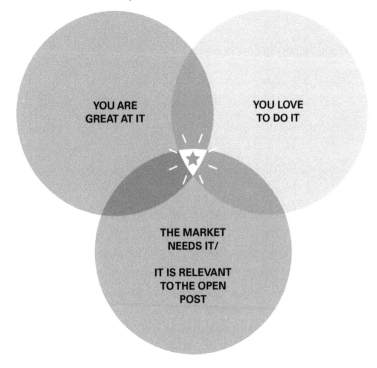

Now it's time to break down the skills you've identified in the sweet spot and develop them into the categories that will form the first page of your functional CV, or FCV. The FCV is different from the conventional CV that lists your previous roles in chronological order, because it builds your career story around what you excel at rather than where you did what. Each category is a high-level skill like communications, strategy, project management, or research and analysis. Define yours using the activities and competencies you've identified.

Next comes the important part, where you drill down on the keywords that you will weave into each of your skills categories. Print out a copy of the job description you are interested in and the job description rewrite tool we covered in Step 6 to reference back to the specific terminology the hiring manager is using to describe the tasks, activities and skills relating to the position. Map those words or phrases against your four skills categories. This is the language that will help you translate what you do into what the organization wants to hire when you start crafting your accomplishment statements in Step 8.

KEY POINTS

In this step, we looked at the importance of:

- how to translate your skills for a mission-driven role;
- the type of skills that are in demand in the purpose economy;
- how to evaluate and map your skills.

What's next?

This step was all about proving your skills by identifying what the market wants and aligning it with what you love doing and what you're great at. You should now have clarified which of your skills fall in the sweet spot, defined your four main skills categories, and harvested the keywords and phrases that the hiring manager is using. Now it's time to build the key-word-rich, tangible and impressive accomplishment statements that will show them why you're the best person for the job.

References and further reading

Acre, Flag, and Carnstone Partners (2018) [accessed 4 December 2019] *The CR and Sustainability Salary Survey 2018* [Online] crsalarysurvey. com/home (archived at https://perma.cc/7Y75-7A4R)

Bradberry, T (2020) [accessed 26 February 2020] The massive benefits of boosting your emotional intelligence, *World Economic Forum*, 17 February [Online] www.weforum.org/agenda/2020/02/emotional-intelligence-career-life-personal-development/ (archived at https://perma.cc/2PL9-3A2Z)

GreenBiz Group (2018) [accessed 4 December 2019] *State of the Profession 2018* [Online] www.greenbiz.com/report/state-profession-2018-report (archived at https://perma.cc/AK7Q-7ZPW)

Houde, S (2017) [accessed 15 September 2020] *Do You Have the Top 5 Sustainability Skills to Survive?*, netimpact.com (archived at https://perma.cc/6LLK-UD9B) [Online] https://www.netimpact.org/blog/future-proof-for-2020-do-you-have-the-top-5-sustainability-skills-to-survive (archived at https://perma.cc/8VFE-H3QG)

Pate, D (2020) [accessed 26 February 2020] *The Skills Companies Need Most in 2020 – And How to Learn Them*, LinkedIn, 13 January [Online] learning.linkedin.com/blog/top-skills/the-skills-companies-need-most-in-2020and-how-to-learn-them (archived at https://perma.cc/73KE-5E2F)

Wow them on paper

What are the best bits of my story that make me unique for the purpose economy?

Did you skip straight to this step? You wouldn't be the first person to succumb to the temptation to get right to 'the good stuff'. But be careful: skipping directly to CV-writing can undermine your results. You first need to be clear on your target audience, what they are buying, and what you are selling to them in a story format that does the work for the hiring manager.

If you have in fact completed Steps 1 through 7, then you're ready! You've done the foundational work that will help you convey why you're so amazing.

Why this step is important

We will cover all elements of writing a killer CV here in a fresh and innovative way. At the same time, we will keep the format simple and clean. We'll cover the dos and don'ts of CV writing from a recruiter's point of view, along with the myths of good CV writing. This step will help you turn your accomplishments into powerful, relevant and compelling statements that will keep the hiring manager on the page longer.

> **TIP** Do the work for them
>
> It is the reader's perception, and not your intention, that controls the fate of your résumé… it is not their job to make sense out of your life.

Myths of CV writing

There are a lot of myths circulating in the jobs market about CV writing, and they can often hobble a candidate's chances of landing a position, even when they're well suited to the role.

Myth 1: CV content should be copied and pasted into LinkedIn

Not exactly. LinkedIn is a powerful tool, so we need to be very careful how we use it. The world – including head-hunters and recruiters – can now access us there. Because LinkedIn doesn't give us the opportunity to customize our profile depending on who's viewing it, it's even more important to take a focused approach to how we position ourselves in our online profile.

While you definitely want to copy and paste some of the content from your CV – especially things like the titles of previous roles – you don't want the entire kitchen sink in there. Your LinkedIn profile can be a bit more friendly and informal than your CV (using the first person 'I'), but it should also be quite a bit shorter. Focus on elevator pitch-style summaries and use keywords in your by-line so that you come up in the search when recruiters are looking for candidates. The by-line is not just your title from your current role, but rather, a personal brand statement. In Step 11, we'll work through the intricacies of crafting a compelling LinkedIn profile.

Myth 2: Hiring managers spend five minutes reading a CV

Nope, they don't! I hate to say it, but all those hours you put into crafting your résumé, all the agonizing and reading and re-reading are worth about 40 seconds of the hiring manager's attention. This means that you need to communicate very quickly the reasons why they should *keep* reading. If you do that successfully, you might get another two minutes.

In the initial stages of recruitment when the hiring manager is whittling down applications into the short list for interviews, they won't read the majority of content in your CV. Readability, white space, and clear accomplishment statements make it easier for the recruiter to get a sense of your unique selling point (USP). Huge blocks of text do not. Your CV is not the place to throw in your entire autobiography!

Myth 3: Special styles and fonts make you stand out

Again, no! A lot of jobseekers are looking for new and different ways to highlight their individuality and unique skills, and there are a lot of graphically designed CV tools online to help you do this. But I would say that these types of CVs only supplement a traditional CV. Don't use special styles and fonts to stand out; rather, go for something that's very simple and easy on the eye. Using **bold** to showcase the names of companies you have worked with (not for) as partners or stakeholders is a nice use of font to help the reader quickly see the diversity of players with whom you've had experience. In this process, name dropping is considered not only okay, but necessary.

Myth 4: You need one CV that works for all positions

Sort of. You will need one CV that works for most positions, and that's going to correlate to what's on LinkedIn, but it will be necessary to customize up to a maximum of around 20 per cent of it for each application. If you have done your targeting well in Step 3, you will be able to build one template CV that works most of the time. It will need slight tweaking to match some keywords your target audience uses, but your overarching personal story and skill categories will stay the same.

Myth 5: CVs should include everything you've ever done

Many people worry about gaps in dates, but the extent to which you should obsess about it depends on where you are in your career. If you're later in your career and you've got 10-plus years' experience, it's likely that what you did early in your career isn't going to be as relevant to a new job as your most recent roles. It's not necessary to spell out all the detail of roles that aren't relevant – instead, you may want to collapse some roles together and include a one-liner just to cover the dates. The investment we are making in building a tight storyline for your CV is designed to help the reader see quickly how you are a perfect match. If we include everything you have ever done, the reader will get overwhelmed and move on to another candidate.

Myth 6: References, sports and hobbies are a part of every CV

This is a good one. I've heard people say, 'I got a job because I put down that I was a triathlete and the hiring manager was also a triathlete, and that's how I got the interview.' That's great, and it's important to build a personal connection with the hiring manager, but I would only put down sports, hobbies and interests if you have some sort of achievement to associate with them. For example, if you're a runner, I don't really care. But if you ran the New York City Marathon, that might be more interesting. If you ran it three times and raised money for charity, that's even more impressive!

You don't need to worry about references, and you don't need to say that they're available on request because that's assumed. It isn't necessary to go into the reference part of the hiring process until you're at the contract negotiation stage, and your list will be in a separate document.

Four-line profile

Personal profiles are the bane of a human resources manager's life. How can so many words communicate so little? A hiring executive has about 30 seconds to extract the key facts from your CV, and if the time runs out and they're still looking, you can expect to land in the reject pile. So why, oh why, dear jobseeker, would you want to make it hard for them to see why you're perfect for the role?

At the same time, personal profiles are the bane of a job-seeker's life. Describing yourself and your achievements is about as fun as listening to a toddler sing 'The Wheels on the Bus' over and over on a long car journey. (Indeed, many people would rather do that than sit down and write 75 words on their employ-ability.) But do it we must, and so we do, reluctantly, and frequently ineffectively. Too often, personal profiles are too verbose and flowery, too full of 'I' statements, too vague, or too long. I've seen them all. But don't lose hope: we're going to work on a fool-proof, pain-free solution to making yours awesome.

Writing a killer personal profile means neatly and succinctly meeting the hiring manager's requirements while staying true to you. A good one will set your CV apart from the hundreds of other sustainability applications pinging their way into their inbox. After all, it's the first place an employer will look for a summary of why you might be a hot candidate, so it's important to nail it.

Does yours say something like this?

'I'm a former events planner with excellent people skills and organizational abilities and a strong passion for sustainability. Having spent ten years in retail, I have a thorough knowledge of the sector, and am committed to using my experience to further the sustainability agenda. I am a fluent French speaker with a recent MBA in Sustainability.'

If it does, it's time to hit delete. Now, let's rewrite it so that you'll get noticed.

First sentence

- *Give yourself a descriptive title.* The market is buying your work experience, so put that first. It can be aspirational. Say your title was 'Events Planner' and you organized events for corporate responsibility (CR) conferences. Now you want to be in marketing and communications within a CR team. You can put in your profile 'CR Marketing Associate', because it does descriptively reflect what you've done, who you are, and where you're going next.
- *Next, look at your total years of experience.* So, 'CR Marketing Associate with five years' experience'.
- *Then home in on the sector.* Give the reader more information on what you know, whom you know, and at what scale your old company was operating. 'CR Marketing Associate with five years' experience shifting mindsets through global communications campaigns and events within matrixed organizations across the energy and retail sectors.'

Second sentence

- *Define yourself with your skills.* What are they? Can you match them up with the job description? Make sure that they're relevant, you can back them up, and they summarize what you've done. Don't be tempted to include an 'I', and certainly never speak in the third person! Think like a headline writer: maximize the space with keywords and forget about the rest.

'Diverse skills in designing multi-stakeholder forums, collaborating with cross-functional teams, and leading cause-related marketing initiatives...'

- *Then drill down on the issues.* What is your knowledge of specific sustainability issues? Environmental? Community investment? Waste? Water? Sustainable supply chain? Human rights? This brings us to: 'Diverse skills in designing multi-stakeholder forums, collaborating with cross-functional teams, and leading cause-related marketing initiatives to build engagement around human rights and youth issues.'

Third and fourth sentences

- *What's your unique selling point?* Make it clear what sets you apart as a candidate for this job. Have you worked abroad? Do you speak languages? Have you recently graduated? Published articles? You could also highlight the countries you have worked in or the leadership roles you have held. 'Fluent in French with cross-cultural experience working and studying in India, France and Brazil', or 'Board member of NGO focused on youth employability', or 'Recent MBA in Sustainable Innovation. Published Author'.

Adding all this up, we get a dynamic personal profile:

'CR Marketing Associate with five years' experience shifting mindsets through global communications campaigns and events within matrixed organizations across the energy and retail sectors. Diverse skills in designing multi-stakeholder forums, collaborating with cross-functional teams, and leading cause-related marketing initiatives to build engagement around human rights and youth issues. Fluent in French with cross-cultural experience working and studying in India, France and Brazil. Board Member of NGO focused on youth employability. Published author.'

Compare the profile above with our original example. *Whom would you hire?*

GENDER MATTERS

I hear time and time again how women often undersell their own career achievements or credit them to others. I also hear that women tend to be stronger champions for others than they are for themselves. Research has found that men overestimate their past performance twice as much as women do (McGregor, 2011). On a related note, a Hewlett Packard report found that men apply for a job when they meet only 60 per cent of the requirements, while women tend only to apply if they meet 100 per cent of the stated job requirements (Mohr, 2014).

As a career coach, I believe that getting the right people into the right roles is the most important factor in individual and organizational success. This starts not with your annual review or a promotion opportunity, but with your initial job application. If you want to reach destination dream job, every step in the journey matters.

---

12 accomplishment statements

Let's step back for a moment. Most jobseekers, no matter their gender, have never been given the language to discuss their accomplishments in a powerful way in their CV. They don't mean to undersell themselves; they just don't have the tools to explain their value to the fullest.

Enter accomplishment statements. Instead of filling your CV with a litany of your previous job responsibilities, use it to highlight your key achievements. This way you can show off and prove the impact that you've had, and relate specific tangible outcomes to the job for which you're applying.

Wondering how to get started? Look over your current CV and try summarizing it into 12 accomplishment statements. Use three statements each to support your four key skill categories from Step 7, for a total of 12 accomplishment statements.

FIGURE 8.1   Accomplishment statement formula

2 5 %   R E S U L T   +   1 0 %   S C O P E   +   6 5 %   S K I L L S

Won $110k new business   over six months from retail and FMCG

clients   through identifying Walmart and PnG needs, writing

proposals, and delivering pitch presentations to   four   Directors.

IMPRESSIVE ACTION VERB –THE SO WHAT? WHY DID THEY PAY YOU?	#S, $/£, MONTHS, COUNTRIES, SIZE OF TEAM	WHAT YOU ACTUALLY DID, HOW YOU DELIVERED THAT RESULT, SKILLS

A good accomplishment statement has four elements:

1 Start with an engaging action verb that translates for the reader why your employer paid you to do this.
2 Include the result or impact of your action (specific numbers, financial value, companies, awards, etc).
3 Include the scope where possible (number of clients served, amount of time invested, etc).
4 End with a description of what tasks you actually performed, specifically including the skills you used.

Figure 8.1 shows the formula for a well-constructed accomplishment statement.

This is typically the hardest thing for jobseekers to do, because it's very hard for people to think about why their employer paid them to do something and what the wider impact was on others. Ask yourself: 'Why did I do this? Why am I proud of this? What was the benefit that my work produced?' Then put that down on paper so it's crystal clear.

Your accomplishment statement should always meet the test we discussed in the last step: it should sit in the sweet spot, the intersection of what you're great at, what you love doing, and what the market needs.

Consider the following examples. The 'before' examples represent the typical content of CVs out there in the marketplace that enumerate jobs and responsibilities. The 'after' examples rework the information into our accomplishment statement format. Which do you find more compelling?

Before: Supported new business development activities including writing proposals and presentations to prospective clients wanting help with sustainability.

After: Won £80k of new sustainability consulting contracts over six months from retail and fast-moving consumer goods (FMCG) clients by identifying **Walmart** and **Procter & Gamble's** needs, writing proposals, and delivering pitch presentations to four directors.

Before: Influenced and inspired company's businesses at C-suite and board levels to understand and act upon the connection between sustainability and commercial growth.

After: Led ground-breaking aviation working group for three airlines to achieve joint commercial-scale uptake of low-carbon renewable jet fuel by organizing inaugural meeting in San Francisco and collaborating across 10 global stakeholders for funding.

Before: Helped to grow payroll giving programme into leading level in United Kingdom and winning a prestigious award by government.

After: Grew payroll giving scheme into United Kingdom's largest with more than 47,000 weekly donors, and won the Treasury Department's gold charter mark by creating employee incentives, branding the programme and improving reporting.

Hopefully you can see how much more substantial and captivating the accomplishment statements are. They transform your CV into an alluring case for hiring you!

> **KEY POINTS**
>
> In this step, we covered:
>
> - myths about CV writing;
> - how to frame your story in terms of accomplishments; and
> - how to craft a strong CV for the impact sector.

What's next?

Now that you've got your CV ready to stop them in their tracks, it's time to craft a cover letter that can accompany it in style.

References and further reading

Houde, S (2014) [accessed 15 September 2020] *Don't Undersell Your Achievements on Your Resume*, LinkedIn [Online] https://www.linkedin.com/pulse/20141110185105-5290176-stop-underselling-your-achievements-on-your-resume (archived at https://perma.cc/M5L7-F5NS)

Houde, S [accessed 15 September 2020] *Build Your CV's Personal Profile To Get an Edge in the Sustainability Jobs Market*, Walk of Life Coaching [Online] https://walkoflifecoaching.com/build-your-cvs-personal-profile-to-get-an-edge-in-the-sustainability-jobs-market/ (archived at https://perma.cc/Q6YM-8QVY)

Houde, S [accessed 15 September 2020] *Busting the Myths of CV and Resume Writing*, Walk of Life Coaching [Online] https://walkoflife-coaching.com/busting-the-myths-of-cv-resume-writing/ (archived at https://perma.cc/3BPQ-LQUK)

McGregor, J (2011) [accessed 6 December 2019] Yet another explanation for why fewer women make it to the top, *Washington Post*, 29 November [Online] www.washingtonpost.com/blogs/post-leadership/post/yet-another-explanation-for-why-fewer-women-make-it-to-the-top/2011/04/01/gIQA2IIP9N_blog.html (archived at https://perma.cc/ULQ6-EXKK)

Mohr, T S (2014) [accessed 6 December 2019] Why women don't apply for jobs unless they're 100% qualified, *Harvard Business Review*, 25 August [Online] hbr.org/2014/08/why-women-dont-apply-for-jobs-unless-theyre-100-qualified (archived at https://perma.cc/JFU5-9AWZ)

Richardson, D (2013) [accessed 15 September 2020] *Skeptical Resume Reader Tells How He Really Thinks*, IMDiversity [Online] https://imdiversity.com/villages/career/skeptical-resume-reader-tells-how-he-really-thinks/ (archived at https://perma.cc/97FG-SH6C)

Write a cover letter using KISS

This sector loves storytelling

Now that you've transformed your CV for maximum effect, it's time for us to take on the dreaded cover letter. Let's face it: it's not much fun to write one, nor usually to read one.

Why this step is (still) important

Cover letters are slowly becoming obsolete. In the age of Twitter, blogs, and text messages, few hiring managers or recruiters have the time or interest to slog through dense text covering more than a page. Many hiring managers no longer require cover letters, instead asking for a writing sample or a short statement of purpose. Nevertheless, cover letters are still a requirement in many job listings, and can be an important hook for drawing a hiring manager's attention if composed correctly. A good cover letter is the executive summary of your whole career story as relevant to your reader and the position you're pursuing, and it's your chance to show off your writing skills and a bit of your personality. It can be a powerful tool in crafting your personal brand and persuading a hiring manager that they should consider you for the position they're filling.

The 'KISS' method – keep it short and sweet

Modern communication mediums are all about brevity, and cover letters are no exception – they should be one page with lots of white space and short sentences, preferably one-line bullet points. The goal is to make it easy for hiring managers to find key information, and to highlight your personality while establishing a personal connection to the organization.

There are three reasons to keep your cover letter short and sweet. We've already covered the first: that hiring managers spend less than a minute on their first pass through an application. You need to make it easy for the eye to find essential information. This means using simple formatting and fonts, leaving lots of white space, and breaking up the text with bullets and section headers.

Second, your cover letter is where you show off your communication skills. In this era of tweets and texts, hiring managers expect us to write concise, convincing, newsworthy content now more than ever. For sustainability roles especially, communication skills are at the top of the list for most of the roles posted. Wow them with punchy, pithy, conversational language, and they may actually want to call and talk to you live.

Third, you want your CV to do the work. In the old days, cover letters were necessarily lengthy to prove how applicants' skills and accomplishments fit the job role. CVs have taken over that role, and cover letters are just a formality to summarize key points. A CV should be focused on your impact skills and accomplishments that are relevant to the role for which you're applying, while a cover letter is meant to introduce how you found out about the job, why it's your dream job, and why you love the company, and to briefly summarize three reasons why your skills fit the requirements.

An effective cover letter in the purpose economy:

- references something personal about your connection to the organization, its impact mission, or one of its employees;
- shows off your communication skills;
- briefly summarizes key reasons why your skills fit the job requirements – five is a good number;
- shows personality (as opposed to boring the reader); and
- gives the hiring manager a brief yet relevant snapshot of who you are and why you are mission-driven.

To achieve this, you'll want to flatter and professionally 'flirt', so to speak... without overdoing it, of course! Take a walk in the hiring manager's shoes and figure out what they do well and what their pain points are. Unlike a CV, it's fine and even encouraged to use the first-person 'I' in a cover letter. Just don't overdo it.

Flatter them by demonstrating that you know something about them, and what they need help with. If you don't know, do more research on the company and the person, then make an educated guess. Remember to mirror their language.

Flirt a bit to make the reader want to meet you, using natural language that shows your personality. Try thinking of it as a kind of love letter, to win their hearts and show you've got game! In the purpose economy, this is where you want to convey your passion for the organization's mission or sustainability efforts. Make sure you have read their sustainability report from front to back first.

Your letter should include the following elements:

- *the hook:* why you're attracted to them;
- *the problem:* how you really get them;
- *the solution:* why they need you;

- *leave them wanting more:* a personalized closing sentence that makes them want to call you.

When I applied for a job at a women's clothing brand, I wrote the CFO a love letter about my proven passion for sustainable fashion and love of their brand. Luckily for me, she had attended the same university, so I mentioned that personal connection as well. Even though I had never been an accountant before, only a bookkeeper for a small company, I studied up on how to do a bank reconciliation and was able to pass the practical test part of the interview. Before I knew it, I was relocating to San Francisco from Washington, DC for my dream job.

TIP

It may not feel relevant to you, but never underestimate how much a fellow alum will feel connected just because you went to the same school or university! If you do happen to have this kind of connection, make sure to highlight it in your cover letter.

Five steps to a winning cover letter

Let's break down the steps to bringing your cover letter to life and making it memorable. First, we need to dispel a common myth: 'I should use a generic greeting at the start of my cover letter.'

Nope!

Recruiters will skim your cover letter for anything that could be disqualifying. This includes typos, a generic salutation (we discussed in Step 6 how to find a real person), or a vibe so non-specific that it reeks of find-replace. I know it seems a bit harsh, but when a hiring manager sees any one of these things, they'll read it as, 'I didn't bother to take my time with this, and I don't *really* care about working here.' Above all, do your research and be specific.

Before launching into your cover letter, you'll always want to complete the job description rewrite we covered in Step 6. Your ability to be specific and to mirror the organization's language hinges on that exercise. Have the rewrite in front of you as you begin your cover letter.

Step 1: Write a specific greeting. As we noted above, 'Dear Sir or Madam' or 'To Whom It May Concern' doesn't cut it. Always find a name. LinkedIn makes this so easy now, which we'll discuss further in Step 11.

Step 2: Write three or four lines to capture the reader's interest, using an authentic and conversational voice. Where did you hear about the position? Why do you stand out as the best candidate? Why do you want to work for their organization? Briefly tell them what you're looking for, and how you would add value.

*Example: Although I can't afford a Tesla yet, I get out of bed in the morning with a passion to fundamentally reduce carbon and waste, and to drive game-changing sustainability initiatives across a global innovator in transportation. I was thrilled when Citi's AVP of Corporate Sustainability, **insert name**, suggested that I apply to the Sustainability Specialist posting on your website.*

Step 3: The bulk of your letter – half a page at maximum – should be in bullet points. These should be distinct from your CV in that they are just one line each, and they summarize your accomplishments rather than drilling down on details.

Example: As a recognized leader in sustainability and supply chain best practice within manufacturing, the impact of my influence has been celebrated through four career achievements. I was selected to be:

- *featured in **James Cameron's** Emmy-nominated climate change docu-series, Years of Living Dangerously;*
- *featured in a **Showtime Network** climate change documentary for auditing **The Honest Company** on energy, water and*

waste, and presented to co-founders Jessica Alba and Chris Gavigan;

- *trained by* **Al Gore** *to deliver his* **Climate Reality Project** *presentation to increase awareness across communities;*
- *co-chair of* **The Earth Institute** *Leadership Council under Jeffrey Sachs.*

Step 4: Write a short sentence to reiterate why they should choose you, followed by supporting bullet points. It's sometimes easiest to write this sentence by telling a friend or family member in plain language, and having them write it for you.

> **Example:** *In addition, my five years of hands-on experience managing organizational sustainability issues such as green manufacturing, waste, green building, and procurement across diverse sectors makes me a perfect fit for your requirements:*

- *LEED AP BD+C certified and Global Reporting Initiative G4 trained;*
- *saved $200k+ in energy and water consumption;*
- *won the manufacturer contracts that led Marriott International to source 75 per cent of their furniture, fixtures and equipment responsibly;*
- *boosted employee morale and saved $200k+ by surveying 1,000+ staff and creating Go Green Committee;*
- *implemented sustainability strategy for $50k client;*
- *saved more than $350k in operating costs and 3,400 metric tons of CO_2 emissions per year.*

Step 5: Close with confidence, competence, and genuine interest in the organization, reinforcing how you will add value to the team relating to their specific skills requirements.

> **Example:** *I can't wait to hear more about Tesla's ongoing growth and how I can drive its sustainability programme's compliance, development and engagement forward.*

Before you hit send

Once you're happy with your cover letter, there are a few more things to do before you send it off.

First, have someone else edit your cover letter. It's very hard to see our own mistakes, even for the best of writers. We tend to see what we intended, rather than what we actually wrote. A good editor is worth their weight in gold! If you are forced to rely on your own devices, it's best to print out your draft so that you stand a better chance of spotting your errors. Another trick is to save the draft in a separate file, then change the font to something completely different from the original. Both approaches help our eyes to spot typos.

Second, check your formatting:

- Use the same letterhead and font style to match your CV.
- Use bold headings and bullet points, not bulky paragraphs.
- A cover letter should be formatted like a formal business letter, depending on the standard format in your country.

Case Study Mariana Souza

Mariana finished her MBA in Sustainability at Bard. She used her MBA projects to help land a job in KPMG's Power and Utilities segment, where she and her team now provide management consulting to clients. Reflecting on the process, Mariana said, 'Cover letters have always been such a drag! These exercises made me rethink the way I can use a cover letter to help clearly communicate my personal story and show some personality, instead of just ticking the box on a job application.'

KEY POINTS

In this step, we covered:

- the relevance of a cover letter in the modern jobs market; and
- how to write a compelling cover letter using the KISS method.

What's next?

Now that we've transformed your CV and worked through the process of writing a compelling cover letter, we'll move into the final stages of stepping into the sustainability jobs market. In Step 10, we'll focus on writing a personal biography in story format.

Reference

Houde, S [accessed 15 September 2020] *3 Reasons to Keep Cover Letters Short and Sweet, Like Tweets*, Walk of Life Coaching [Online] https://walkoflifecoaching.com/3-reasons-to-keep-cover-letters-short-and-sweet-like-tweets/acre (archived at https://perma.cc/6J5E-3ARZ)

PART FOUR

Step into the market

Tell me so I'll listen

How do I convert my unique story into a thought leader's biography?

It can be overwhelming to try to express a competitive advantage in the crowded, noisy, unstructured impact jobs market. A well-crafted CV and cover letter, while essential, is no longer enough. In this step, we'll walk through the process of telling a powerful career story in punchy language that drills down on your unique selling point (USP), making it easy for a hiring manager to get a sense of what sets you apart from hundreds of other candidates.

Why this step is important

The most powerful tool for this type of storytelling is a biography, but writing a great bio is a challenge for most jobseekers. This step will help you to put your best foot forward when networking, rather than simply shopping your CV all over the place, and risking coming across as desperate or unfocused. We'll cover how to compose your biography using a clear formula, when to use different kinds of bios, and how to convert a bio into a LinkedIn summary.

Narratives are what spark the imagination. This step will empower you to weave themes out of facts in a prose that's readable, relatable and – most important – memorable.

Crafting your story

Recruiters and hiring managers are suffering from information fatigue. Can you blame them? CVs, LinkedIn profiles, internal job application forms, bios, Twitter feeds, and references... It's crazy out there in the post-information age. There's just too much of it!

So, as a jobseeker trying to express your own competitive advantage, what do you do? First, resist the temptation to try to dazzle hiring managers with an avalanche of bare facts and figures. Instead, entice them with a good story, just as sustainability practitioners have to do with their stakeholders. Making it easy for a hiring manager to get a sense of your career story will set you apart from the hundreds of other candidates, which is why being a great storyteller is so important if you're on the hunt for your next role.

FINDING YOUR STORY

Before we explore the tools for telling an authentic, effective career story that conveys real passion, relatable experiences and demonstrable skillsets, we must first drill down on the three most important considerations in marketing yourself:

- *Know your audience.* This is what makes you relevant to the employer – it's about knowing what the market wants.

- *Know your skills.* This is what helps you to be confident in what you're selling – it's about knowing what you're great at and being able to prove it.

- *Know your passions.* This is what sets you apart – it's about knowing where you want to have an impact and why.

Take a pen and a blank sheet of paper and write down the words that come to mind under each of these headings. Use colour, draw pictures, get creative and brainstorm!

Once you've got your responses ready, it's time to start thinking about how you can string them all together into a coherent narrative. Ask yourself: what's the common theme? What's the one conceptual thread that will help you tie it all together?

This exercise is crucial in laying the groundwork for the personal branding tools that you'll put out into the impact marketplace.

In completing the above exercise, you bypass the information overload that's plaguing employers by crafting a compelling story out of your history.

A biography is a powerful networking tool. It puts you on your front foot as a commodity, rather than on your back foot as a desperate-seeming jobseeker shoving a CV down someone's inbox. It says, 'Look at my credentials, my story, my journey and my gravitas... you need to talk to me.' It can also be used for website marketing materials and for public speaking.

Importantly, there are different types of biographies for different purposes.

THE FOUR BIOS EVERY JOBSEEKER NEEDS

Contrary to popular belief, you don't need one biography – you need four:

1 a 160-character micro-biography for Twitter;

2 a short bio to serve as the four-line profile in your CV (we first discussed this in Step 8);

3 a full bio that's no more than 2,000 characters long and written in the third person; and

4 a LinkedIn bio that's 2,000 characters or fewer and written in the first person for the About section of your LinkedIn profile. (We'll cover this more in the next step.)

Each of these is simply a narrative version of the information you would include in your CV, albeit sliced, chiselled, and buffed to fit into different formats. You are not crafting four distinct bios – you are providing different levels of detail of the same information to keep your personal branding consistent. They build upon each other.

The full biography

Let's start with your full biography. It should be more formal than your other bios, and is really helpful to use when you're networking by email and sending your entire CV could come across as a bit too desperate. You can also use this bio if you're speaking at an event, or for inclusion on a website. This one is the story of you.

Aim for about half a page in length with an 11-point font, and remember to write in the third person (for example, 'Shannon is' rather than 'I am'). Your full bio should be no more than 2,000 characters long.

Start with your name and insert a small professional photo in the top left corner (preferably the same one that is on LinkedIn), then get down to business. State what you do and get your key accomplishments in there early to hook the reader. Include only impressive and relevant information, such as your current job, professional experience, publications, presentations, professional memberships, awards, honours, certifications and education.

Include a brief final comment about where you live or your favourite activities, but no more than that.

ESCHEW ADJECTIVES

Myth – Jobseekers should include descriptive words in their bio to make it more interesting.

Adjectives are alright in moderation, as you do want to write an interesting story about your career journey, but 98 per cent of your bio should be factual. Limit descriptive words to your transitions between roles or careers.

You want to tell it like a story, an impressive journey that you have been navigating through your career to date, but without wittering on for pages; for example, you might say, 'Ananya chose a career in social responsibility after seeing the poverty on the streets of Mumbai as a teenager...,' but you would then jump right into what the roles (titles and companies) were in your career in social responsibility.

Once you've got the bones of your bio together, arrange it into the following four categories:

PART 1: THE PITCH

The first 100 words of your bio are your sales pitch, so use them to set out your story in neat, punchy language that drills down on your unique selling point (USP). They are your mission, your goal, your passion for your purpose-driven work. Hook the reader here. Think of this part as your 30-second elevator pitch.

This first paragraph is crucial to getting a recruiter's attention, so make sure the key information is up front and unmissable. Many people are too shy to set out their career expectations somewhere as public as LinkedIn, but stating what you're looking for from your next job – in terms of dream role, dream company or both – can be a smart move that makes you look dynamic, ambitious and strategic.

PART 2: YOUR SPECIALITIES

The second part of your bio is your list of specialities. This part is all about optimizing your profile for search using relevant keywords, so think of it as an advertisement to tell all your potential employers how much they need you.

Your specialities should be a list of at least 10 terms that cover all your industries, skills and interests, as well as past, current and potential job titles. Make sure you include synonyms (ie 'sustainability' *and* 'corporate social responsibility' *or* 'corporate responsibility') to make sure you capture any keywords that might be important to the reader.

PART 3: YOUR ACHIEVEMENTS

The achievement section is my favourite part of a jobseeker's profile, because it's the place where you let your track record do the talking. This is not the place to be modest or shy about your achievements. Why are you proud of that accomplishment? If you don't tell the world how amazing you are, who else will?

Just keep in mind, though, that a bio should be limited to one or two key achievements. Unlike the CV, which goes into 12 accomplishments in detail, that much information would be unwieldy in a bio.

PART 4: YOU'RE UNIQUE

The final part of your profile is the place to mention your qualifications, volunteer leadership, interests and activities. Take the opportunity to inject a little of yourself into your profile – but do it in a strategic way by keeping in mind the kind of keywords recruiters might be searching for, while making the reader smile. It's good to end on a happy note, and a bit of well-placed humour is always memorable!

Make sure to keep modifying your biography, and update it periodically to keep it fresh and to reflect changes in your achievements. My friend 'Lucy's' biography provides a great example. I've changed her name and some of her details, because she doesn't want anyone to get the wrong idea and think she's looking to change jobs!

Lucy is a Global Sustainability Director & Social Innovation Intrapreneur at Acme who has spent 15 years creating new circular business models and products that integrate social, environmental and commercial goals across the consumer packaged goods (CPG), retail and plastics sectors.

Lucy transformed one of the largest risks at Acme into a growth opportunity through new technologies and investments, securing spend from $4 million to $40 million and building a global team of 20. She also spearheaded shifting the Acme Foundation from philanthropic to business strategic, building a culture of intrapreneurship through jointly founding Acme Impact Fund and growing it from $300,000 to $5 million. As a board member, she selected 25 projects over three years and designed shared value criteria – inputs, outputs and impacts to improve measurement.

Previously, Lucy held roles in marketing, competitive intelligence and sales. Prior to her current role, Lucy was a Product Manager responsible for pricing in South Europe, the Middle East and Africa, based in Switzerland. During her undergraduate degree, Lucy worked for RunFast athletic shoe company focusing on competitive analysis.

Lucy was recognized as one of the industry's Top Women Breaking the Mold in 2017. She frequently speaks about plastic waste issues and solutions at GreenBiz, USAID and Our Ocean, and has been published in Sustainable Brands *and* The Guardian.

Giving back using her leadership skills, Lucy has served as Hunger Relief board member for the Houston Food Bank, co-founding the Montgomery County Produce Rescue Center for the largest food bank network in the USA. She has volunteered as a business consultant for an AIDS orphanage in rural South Africa and a start-up medical clinic benefiting genocide orphans in Rwanda.

Lucy holds an MBA from the University of Texas McCombs School of Business as well as a BS in International Marketing and minor in International Economics from Clemson University. She is passionate about using business as a force for good to solve social and environmental challenges and has completed Harvard Business School's Creating Shared Value Leadership Program.

The LinkedIn biography

Your LinkedIn bio uses all the same ingredients as your full bio above, but it adds in a little sprinkle of personality, too. It should be written in the first person in a conversational, friendly-but-business tone in 2,000 characters – no more, and certainly no less! I prefer to read each sentence as a separate paragraph, forcing you to keep things quite punchy and avoid the long paragraphs that turn off a social media reader. We'll spend more time on your LinkedIn profile when we get to Step 11, but for now, here's Lucy's example again to help you see the differences between each type of biography:

Using job for good: Plastic trash to bricks. Plastics waste to roads. Plastic junk to fuel. Plastics back to plastics. Driving innovation and investment to create new technology that scales the circular life of plastics into profits while lifting people out of poverty. Inventing new systems and infrastructure to turn plastic waste into an infinite resource.

With 14 years of packaging experience, I've been embedding triple bottom line strategies across the consumer packaged goods (CPG), retail and plastics sectors.

Partners include:

- *[list of partner companies];*
- *Circulate Capital, Recycling Partnership, Ocean Conservancy, the Alliance to End Plastic Waste.*

Some of my career achievements include:

- *recognized as a courageous leader through the Top Women Breaking the Mold industry award;*

- *designed integrated End Use (B2B) Marketing organization by delivering $100 million growth;*
- *mitigated greatest business risk related to plastics by increasing spend ten-fold and building a high-profile global team of 20 from leading brands and NGOs;*
- *spearheaded shifting the Acme Foundation from philanthropic to business strategic;*
- *built a culture of intrapreneurship through jointly founding and growing the Acme Impact Fund to $5 million;*
- *pioneered global innovation lab to integrate packaging from pellet to second-life.*

I frequently speak about plastic waste issues and solutions at GreenBiz, USAID, and Our Ocean and have been published in Sustainable Brands *and* The Guardian.
Volunteering and personal:

- *served as Hunger Relief board member for the Houston Food Bank; co-founding the Montgomery County Produce Rescue Center for the largest food bank network in the USA;*
- *business consultant for an AIDS orphanage in rural South Africa and a start-up medical clinic benefiting genocide orphans in Rwanda.*

When I'm not saving the world from plastic waste, my home is in Houston, Texas. I can also be spotted escaping to hike mountains every chance I get.

The CV and Twitter biographies

We already covered in Step 8 how to craft the short, four-line biography that appears at the top of your CV in the profile section. Here's Lucy's example:

Global Sustainability Director & Social Innovation Intrapreneur with 14 years' experience developing new circular business models and products that integrate social, environmental and commercial goals across the consumer packaged goods (CPG), retail and plastics sectors. Influences C-suite, shifts mindsets at industry forums, and builds system change coalitions to address poverty across a circular economy. Cross-cultural team leadership and volunteering in the United States, Switzerland, South Africa, Rwanda and the UK. Board member.

Values: Shared value. Solution seeker. Ethical leadership. Faithful. Global mindset.

Traits: Creative thinker. Courageous team leader. Positive energy. Change maker. Adventurous.

To shorten things even further into a micro-biography for Twitter as your headline under your name, you will generally condense the first sentence or two from your LinkedIn headline and 'About' section. You should maximize Twitter's 160-character limit. On that platform, remember that you can abbreviate and use symbols (such as & instead of 'and') to squeeze the most information possible into a small space. You can also be a bit pithy here. The trick is to distil your essence into this very short form. Here's Lucy's example:

Global sustainability leader, social innovation intrapreneur, circular economy expert, transformer of plastic waste into infinite resource while promoting prosperity

---

Case Study Chantal Beaudoin

Chantal Beaudoin has worked as a sustainability change maker for 15 years, planning and implementing large-scale organizational strategy and programmes. She made her move into the corporate sphere after more than a decade working primarily in higher education, becoming a sustainability consultant at McDonald's Ltd. Reflecting on her work crafting her bio, Chantal said, 'By the end of this process, I was able to re-frame my experience. I sculpted a bio that was relevant for a more corporate audience and engaged them in my career story. It gave me the confidence to make the career move I was aiming for.'

> **KEY POINTS**
>
> In this step, we covered:
>
> - how to craft your personal brand story for various purposes; and
> - how to write the four different types of biographies you'll need for the modern impact jobs market.

What's next?

Now that we've written your story, let's shift to working on how best to build it online.

References and further reading

Houde, S (2014) [accessed 15 September 2020] *Dear Shannon, How Can I Make My Bio Social Media Friendly*, GreenBiz [Online] https://www.greenbiz.com/article/dear-shannon-how-can-i-make-my-bio-social-media-friendly (archived at https://perma.cc/BKF2-87ZJ)

Houde, S [accessed 14 September 2020] *LinkedIn Checklist for Sustainability Jobseekers*, Walk of Life Coaching [Online] https://walkoflifecoaching.com/linkedin-checklist-for-sustainability-jobseekers/ (archived at https://perma.cc/H72V-NF7C)

Sustainability jobs are all about partnering

How can I show I'm someone worth collaborating with on LinkedIn?

N etworking is the single most important aspect of a job-seeker's process. While face-to-face contact is certainly ideal, there is no better tool out there to supercharge your networking strategy than LinkedIn. It is by far the most effective way to connect (and reconnect) with your existing contacts, organically grow your professional network and come to potential employers' attention.

Why this step is important

Many people think that LinkedIn is only for jobseekers and recruiters. In fact, it is one of the most powerful tools available to build relationships and networks, raise funding and increase brand awareness – whether your personal brand or your company's. These days, a well-optimized LinkedIn profile is a must-have for any jobseeker or professional in the impact space. Think of LinkedIn like a massive conference or office party. You can find out so much about people and easily reach out to build new relationships. In the impact economy, those connections are indispensable.

Then, of course, most recruiters will use LinkedIn to vet job candidates. However, many jobseekers aren't on the platform at all, or don't use it to its fullest potential. According to Jobvite (2018), LinkedIn is the channel recruiters use most, with 77 per cent of them saying they used it in 2018 compared with 63 per cent who used Facebook. Notably, that represents a significant decline from 2017, when 92 per cent of recruiters said they used LinkedIn. Recruiters are increasingly using Instagram to find job candidates, especially younger recruiters and those working in the technology sector.

Nevertheless, even as LinkedIn is seeing more competition from newer platforms, it remains a central hub for jobseekers and recruiters. LinkedIn said it had about 660 million users at the end of 2019, the result of explosive growth since its 2003 launch. It is an essential arrow in the jobseeker's quiver.

In this step, we will focus on how to make optimal use of the LinkedIn platform during a job search, and to craft a profile that is attractive to hiring managers and recruiters while also staying true to yourself. This work is a continuation of the journey toward developing a consistent personal brand story.

LINKEDIN DEMOGRAPHICS

According to Heitmann (2019):

- Millennials are the fastest growing segment on LinkedIn, growing at three times the rate of other demographic groups.

- Millennials are twice as likely to change jobs as any other generation.

- Sixty-four per cent of millennials say a good job is 'one they're proud to talk about', underscoring the increased desire for purpose in their work.

A note on dynamic platforms

LinkedIn, like all social media platforms, is dynamic and constantly evolving. The many programmers LinkedIn employ spend their days tweaking and refining the interface and algorithms based on the company's extensive efficacy research and market feedback. Similarly, the prominence of individual social media platforms rises and falls (does anyone remember MySpace?), and LinkedIn may not always be the flagship platform for the jobs market that it is now. As with everything in life, things change and will keep changing. This book was published at a fixed point in time with the most current information available, but it will be up to us as jobseekers to do our own research and determine where differences may have arisen over time.

That being said, there are certain overarching principles that will continue to hold. Most importantly, no matter what social media channel you're on, make sure you're sending a consistent personal branding message, because recruiters will vet you across your entire digital footprint. The world's moving fast, and you need to stay on top of it to maximize your prospects. Google yourself a few times a year to see how you show up. As platforms change, make sure to stay flexible and informed about which will serve you best.

As of 2020, LinkedIn is the professional network of choice for recruiters like me, providing a unique database of impact economy professionals. It's a gold mine for research about companies and people, and for fresh content that could be relevant to those companies and people. That's why we're going to focus on it here. As you read this step, I invite you to keep in mind that while some of the details may grow dated, the principles will endure.

OVERCOMING SOCIAL MEDIA RESISTANCE

I attribute much of my success as a career coach to social media as a marketing platform. I didn't come to it without considerable resistance, though, and you may be feeling the same – especially if you're old enough to have grown up before the internet dominated our lives.

About a year after I launched my business in 2009, Andy Cartland, Acre Resources' managing director, told me I'd better get on Twitter. My response? I was way too busy to be bothered with a little blue bird. I had a website and a decent contact list, what more did I need?

The answer was: quite a lot. My website alone was not enough to maximize my online profile or to attract the traffic I needed to grow my business. And so – with some trepidation – I joined the wider social media world in 2010, and slowly but surely started to see results.

Since then, social media in general, and LinkedIn in particular, have become invaluable to my business for three overarching reasons:

1 It helps me *stay informed* of what's new and hot in my sector, allowing me to play on what others are interested in and stay ahead of the curve.

2 It helps me build my own *brand credibility* through my thought leadership, and to get my voice heard in an increasingly crowded sustainability marketplace. When it comes to work in the impact economy, consistently communicating your passion for and expertise in your issues is essential.

3 It helps me to *connect* with others to nourish my networks and see where my connections are creating impact. Word of mouth is everything!

Setting up an effective LinkedIn account is undeniably time-consuming, but it's worth it. If you're willing to put in the effort to create and maintain your profile and presence, it will help you to realize your impact career goals.

LinkedIn tips

Jobseekers should use LinkedIn as a research tool. The profile you design about who you are and where you're going next needs to consider LinkedIn as your public CV. It should not include as much detail as your actual CV, but the language and messaging around your personal brand needs to be consistent. Here are five tips for using LinkedIn effectively for your sustainability job search.

Tip 1: You only get one chance to make a good impression

Simply creating a profile is not enough to make you stand out to potential employers. You have to grab their attention with a compelling (and relevant) story about who you are and what you do. Jobseekers must first articulate a clear career strategy, because with LinkedIn you can't customize your profile to fit a plethora of job types. It's one size fits all, so aim your compass first and decide exactly what you are selling and to whom.

Tip 2: Keep it short and simple

LinkedIn is not just a digital version of your paper CV. Our attention spans are much shorter online, so make your profile easily digestible by using keywords that impress and avoiding long paragraphs and jargon. Also, more and more recruiters are using LinkedIn to find potential candidates, so optimize your profile for search by using the 'skills and expertise' section to add five to ten keywords that capture who you are and what you're qualified to do.

Tip 3: Think like an advertiser and promote yourself

Think of your LinkedIn profile as an advertisement telling all your potential employers how much they need you. Don't be shy about your achievements – tell the world how amazing you are with compelling text backed up with proven accomplishments. Be sure to solicit recommendations from your current and past colleagues. Nothing sells the product of you better than glowing reviews from people who have worked with you first-hand!

Tip 4: Smile!

While it's important to leverage your LinkedIn profile with relevant and intriguing content, none of that will matter if your photo is scaring off potential employers! You should use a photo that looks professional – ideally a headshot taken with a lens camera by a real photographer. The latest model smart phones also allow for portrait settings, which can be almost as good. If you can't afford to hire a pro, make sure you look natural and approachable with your eyes showing clearly. The background and light will be best if you do it outdoors and have trees or plants behind you to show your sustainability focus. Remember that recruiters, future colleagues, and prospective employers are using this site, so make sure you put your best face forward. According to LinkedIn's own data, profiles with a photo get 21 times the clicks of profiles without, so that picture is clearly important (Ceniza-Levine, 2019).

Tip 5: Work that network

If you want to know someone who knows someone you know, you can reach out to that second connection on LinkedIn and get results more quickly and reliably than through other social media channels. It is like attending a big friend-of-friend conference. This concept is crucial in job searching, as it allows you to engage with human beings, in person or by email, before sending a blind application. That extra connection often makes all the difference in a jobseeker's success.

One of the most valuable aspects of LinkedIn is the ability to browse your extended network for new and interesting connections.

- Go into the profile of one of your most relevant contacts and click 'see all connections' in the bottom right of their page.
- Scan for people in companies, industries, or positions you would like to target, then ask them to connect. Don't do this haphazardly, though, since LinkedIn will suspend your account if too many people complain they don't know you. If you're unsure, add a customized message to the invitation explaining why you'd like to connect.
- Make sure you research their past positions and interests to find some common ground – don't just say you are looking for a job at their company.
- Another way to build your network is by joining groups that you can search for by typing in a keyword into the top right box, like 'CSR' or 'sustainability'. You can also find top groups by looking at people you admire and seeing where they are group members.

From bio to LinkedIn summary

In Step 8, we wrote our four-line profile that goes at the top of a CV. In Step 10, we used that content to build a more complete bio. Now it's time to convert that to a more punchy and friendly LinkedIn summary. Remember that only the first two lines will show at the top of your profile – the reader will have to click to expand the rest, so give them a reason to do so. Here's an example:

> *For more than a decade, I have been ensuring that known consumer brands do the 'right thing' by their suppliers and consumers, as well as the planet. I help brands grow as disruptive market leaders with a competitive advantage around their community and environmental initiatives.*
>
> *As an issues expert in palm oil, coffee, deforestation, packaging, sustainable agriculture and animal welfare, I improve footprints from cradle to grave within the market constraints for profit across the consumer goods, retail and food sectors.*
>
> *Brands include: Dunkin' Brands, Nestlé Waters, Starbucks, T-Mobile, Timberland, ITT, National Wildlife Federation and Harvard University.*

It's a good idea to list companies, clients and stakeholders with whom you have worked here. Contrary to broader social advice, name-dropping in this case is cool and critical!

Elements of a profile

LinkedIn is a dynamic platform, and its elements evolve as its algorithms get more sophisticated and its developers respond to changing user needs. Generally, you want to keep in mind that your LinkedIn profile can be less formal than your CV, and should also be more succinct and focused on key points.

Headline

You have a choice to put either your title and company, or just keywords. Unless your title and organization are going to be compelling to your target audience, it's best to stick to keywords. This is especially true if you are making any kind of job change. Here are some examples of good headlines for sustainability jobseekers:

- *Human Rights in ICT | Public Policy | Government Affairs | Partnerships | Data Privacy | Digital Impact | AI;*
- *Impact Investing | Start-Ups | Sustainable Finance | Renewable Energy | Emerging Markets;*
- *Global Sustainability Director & Social Innovation Intrapreneur | Plastics | Systems Change | Circular Economy.*

About

This is the summary section we just discussed where only the first two lines are visible until the reader expands them, so make those two lines count. Be compelling and intriguing, so that they want to learn more about you. Go on to drop some names of clients or previous employers, then briefly list the best four or five career achievements from your CV. Finish by listing leadership roles, speaking engagements, or other things that set you apart.

In those two, precious first lines, state your mission, purpose, and impact focus clearly and concisely to wow your reader right out of the gate and make them want to expand this section to see more about you. You are allocated 2,000 characters, and you should use the whole space. Weave in keywords recruiters might need to see, but do so as part of the narrative. Don't just list a bunch of terms!

Ultimately, this section is an executive summary, a story board of sorts where you've extracted your five best achievement statements and truncated them into a narrative.

Articles and activity

Recruiters will look at your online thought leadership, as demonstrated through your social media channels. On LinkedIn, these show at the top of your profile, so it's important that you contribute your own content.

Now, perhaps you're not the strongest writer. Certainly, not all impact roles need you to be! Even if you don't post much original work, you can still contribute constructively and thoughtfully by sharing interesting and relevant content with a quick comment of your own to add something to the conversation. The trick here is to maintain a sustained presence, engaging on topics that are especially relevant to your focus area. You don't have to spend hours a day doing it. Indeed, quality is more important than quantity when it comes to your own contributions.

Experience

This part should be about *you*, not the organizations you've worked for! A reader can click on the organization's logo to learn more about it if they want to. This section should highlight you and your skills. After all, that's what you want them to buy into.

This section should not be a mirror image of your CV, but rather provide the most important things you want to tell people about your work history. You may just have a list of client names or stakeholder names for each job, for instance. Above all, don't cut and paste your CV into this section. Not only have you already provided the essentials of your story earlier in your profile, but recruiters also associate excessive detail in this section with less experienced candidates. It can also look a little desperate.

Education

Keep this section clean and simple – there's no need to include every class you attended or every club of which you were a member. Make sure to select your university from the dropdown menu, so that its logo shows.

Volunteer experience

As we discussed in several previous steps, recruiters in the impact space look favourably on volunteer or social engagement work. Try to make sure you list roles that are strategic and skill-building for you, not just painting walls at a school.

Just like your work experience, make sure you include the most salient aspects of your volunteer history in your 'About' section, and don't cut and paste all the details from your CV into this space. Link to the organizations with which you've volunteered, just as you did for your work experience and education.

Recommendations

The more quality recommendations you get on your profile, the better. Having others vouch for you goes a long way, and it's a good idea to ask people to recommend you. (Do it for them, too!) Be selective about who you ask, though, as the source matters. It's best to ask clients or direct line managers, as their views on your performance are most relevant.

Accomplishments

LinkedIn uses this section to encompass just about everything else. It shouldn't be confused with how we defined accomplishment statements for the CV in Step 8. Fill in as much as you can for this section, but only that which is relevant to where you are going next, not everything from your entire career. This is where you share your publications, courses, languages, awards and other additional information that adds colour to your profile. There is no public speaking section so I would lump these in with your publications.

Interests

Recruiters and networking colleagues can see which groups, thought leaders, and companies you follow, and it gives them a good indication of your interests.

> **TIP**   How to increase your profile views
>
> According to LinkedIn software engineers, there are some really basic tricks you can use to get more people to look at your profile (Ceniza-Levine, 2019):
>
> - selecting an industry gets you 30 times more clicks;
> - adding at least five skills gets you 17 times more clicks; and
> - including relevant volunteer work gets you six times more clicks.

LinkedIn checklist

As you build and refine your LinkedIn profile, the following checklist will help you to keep track of your efforts and make sure you've used the platform to optimal effect.

Your profile

PHOTO

- looks like a professional photo, not personal;
- expression is comfortable and approachable, shows personality;
- ideally a headshot taken with a lens camera by a real photographer, or using portrait setting on newer-model smart phones;
- natural, outdoor light is best;
- background a simple sky or trees/plants;
- upload a background photo of something relevant to your interests.

HEADLINE UNDER YOUR NAME

- use these 120 characters to describe industry, skills and objective;
- keywords that a recruiter would need to find you.

ABOUT SECTION

- lead with compelling two lines;
- appealing and relevant story about who you are and what you do;
- weave in keywords that your target audience will be looking for;
- first person, friendly tone, conversational.

Other information

ARTICLES AND ACTIVITY
- share articles relevant to your career strategy.

PROFESSIONAL EXPERIENCE

- use years without months;
- logos of companies showing;
- videos and project examples attached;
- short bullets of achievements – maximum one line;
- relevant achievements to target audience;
- use bullets and spacing to break up text;
- list of key clients;
- list of key sectors;
- skills and expertise for keywords.

EDUCATION, VOLUNTEER EXPERIENCE AND RECOMMENDATIONS, ETC

- university logo, graduation year and degree clearly displayed;
- full list of volunteer and causes experience with logos;

- 10 recommendations from current and past colleagues and clients;
- publications and projects;
- certifications, awards, languages;
- follow relevant thought leaders;
- join relevant groups.

Case Study   Peggy Brannigan

After working in Paris and Amsterdam for 12 years, Peggy Brannigan returned to the Silicon Valley, ultimately joining LinkedIn to lead their global environmental sustainability team and serving as a mentor for Stanford GSB's Center for Social Innovation. Reflecting on her career journey, Peggy said, 'It was a tremendous help to use these guidelines to refine my LinkedIn profile. I was able to present a clear career narrative and had great response from employers reaching out about potential jobs.'

KEY POINTS

In this step, we covered:

- how to use LinkedIn to demonstrate that you're a good partner and collaborator; and
- how to construct your LinkedIn profile and presence to maximum effect in the impact sector.

What's next?

Now that you've got your bio, CV, cover letter and LinkedIn profile in tip-top shape, we'll move on to unpacking some of the myths of working with recruiters and head hunters.

References and further reading

Ceniza-Levine, C (2019) [accessed 27 December 2019] Maximize your LinkedIn profile for job search – tips from recruiters and LinkedIn company insiders, *Forbes*, 24 June [Online] www.forbes.com/sites/carolinecenizalevine/2019/06/24/maximize-your-linkedin-profile-for-job-search-tips-from-recruiters-and-linkedin-company-insiders/#601ca43e1f75 (archived at https://perma.cc/E6D5-27LK)

Heitmann, B (2019) [accessed 8 December 2020] *LinkedIn Has Millions of Jobs and the Right One for You*, LinkedIn Official Blog, 22 April [Online] blog.linkedin.com/2019/april-/22/linkedin-has-20-million-jobs-and-the-right-one-for-you (archived at https://perma.cc/9S8C-TKUH)

Jobvite (2018) [accessed 27 December 2019] *The Tipping Point: The next chapter in recruiting* [Online] www.jobvite.com/wp-content/uploads/2018/11/2018-Recruiter-Nation-Study.pdf (archived at https://perma.cc/9SKT-Y2CS)

Working with recruiters

Where do I find the best impact roles?

Now that we've covered how to optimize a LinkedIn profile for the purpose economy, let's talk about how to work with recruiters. Contrary to popular belief, recruiters work for companies, not candidates. They are not your friends. This step will help jobseekers to navigate the recruitment industry, providing tips and tools to manage these important relationships so that both sides benefit.

Why this step is important

Most jobseekers think they can reach out to recruiters, get their résumé into the database, and wait for the recruiter to call with their dream job. Unfortunately, it doesn't work that way. This step will dispel some of the misconceptions out there, explaining what recruiters will and won't do. It will help jobseekers save time by getting in the head of a recruiter, whether that be a corporate hiring manager within a company or a recruitment consultant within an agency. We'll cover how to make the recruitment process work for us, rather than against us, while managing our expectations.

Tips for approaching recruiters

It's important to remember that a recruiter's main concern is finding the best possible candidate for their client, so they're likely to overlook a CV that's not customized and relevant or an elevator pitch that's not polished. Recruiters really do read more than 100 CVs a day, so a successful jobseeker won't make them work harder to find what they need.

When it comes to approaching sustainability recruitment agencies, these tips will help you get the outcome you want.

Tip 1: Understand what a sustainability recruitment firm actually does

Recruitment agencies are hired by a corporation or organization to identify and recruit candidates with a particular skill and competency set. Their main goal will be to make this exact match and find a shortlist of three to five candidates to put forward for interviews. Many agencies are not 'head hunters', and will not have the time to find each candidate a job. The responsibility remains with the candidate to find the roles online on the recruiter's website.

Here is a short list of what a recruiter will and won't do.

Recruiters won't:

- Spend their time to find you a job – they just don't have that kind of time for every candidate.
- Redesign your CV or cover letter – that's what career coaches are for. A recruiter will definitely not help you with your

personal rebranding. In fact, unlike when you apply directly to a company, recruiters will need to see you meeting almost all the job listing's criteria before they'll even consider you. They don't like career changers who have not put in the effort to demonstrate how their skills and experiences are transferable and relevant to their client, the hiring organization.

- Have unlimited time to help – remember, the hiring company pays them, so you are only valuable to a recruiter if they can place you. Be considerate of a recruiter's limited time.

Recruiters will:

- Help position and sell you to their client if you are qualified for a live role.
- Negotiate salary on your behalf – but only in line with the company's demands.
- Serve as your intermediary in negotiations with the company.

Tip 2: Find a role that is posted on their website for which you are well qualified and competitive

A recruiter will be much more likely to help you if you are applying for a live role, and all executive search firms list their clients' job openings online. Find the one or two roles you are most qualified for, and start by customizing your CV for those roles before applying. Don't expect the recruiter to do this for you. There will usually be an online application process. Nevertheless, after submitting your CV, follow up a few days later with a live call to the appropriate consultant. You should be ready with your elevator pitch for this first call.

Tip 3: Treat all conversations with a recruiter as an interview

Recruiters represent their clients, the company or organization with the open role, and that is how they get paid. They are, in fact, outsourced hiring managers. So, you should treat every conversation you have with a recruiter as an interview. Be ready to sell your top three skills, and summarize your relevant experience in a sentence or two. Also be ready to tell the recruiter why you want this role, and how you are better than the competition. Do your homework on the company first.

Keep in mind, too, that recruiters don't like to see people undervalue themselves. If you do the legwork to translate your accomplishments and skillsets, you can prove that you have enough experience to hit the ground running in a bit of a stretch role.

Tip 4: Follow up

If none of their current roles suit you, most recruiters allow you to submit your CV into their database or LinkedIn network to be considered for future job openings. However, it's important that you check back for updates regularly. Every time recruitment agencies have a new role, they will post it to their site and other job boards such as LinkedIn groups, so register for their weekly bulletin or RSS feed to stay on top of the latest live roles.

Tip 5: Give to receive

A healthy relationship is a two-way street, and your relationship with a recruiter is no exception. Try to get in the head of the recruiter and consider what they want. At the most basic level, they want more business and more clients. Where you're able, offer them business development help as well. For instance, if you can tip them off with leads of what's happening in the market, or what companies may need their services in the future, they will love you. It's also a good idea to refer well-qualified candidates to them for open roles they have, although obviously you don't have to do this for roles you want yourself!

DIVERSITY, EQUITY AND INCLUSION (DEI)

Discrimination in the jobs market – as anywhere else in life – is a long-standing reality. Fortunately, things are starting to change, both at the employer level and among jobseekers and the attributes they look for in an organization.

According to ZipRecruiter's first annual DEI Survey, (Pollak, 2019), the majority of jobseekers look for employers with a commitment to DEI. The recruiting firm found that millennial and Generation X jobseekers are more likely to value workplace diversity in the job search than other generations, compared with other criteria such as salary and flexible work options. Survey results also showed that millennial jobseekers are likely to double their average tenure at a given company if that company is committed to DEI.

Research shows that a commitment to DEI can boost business outcomes. For example, a 2019 analysis by the *Wall Street Journal* (Holger, 2019) found that the 20 most diverse S&P 500 firms financially outperformed the index's non-diverse firms over both five- and 10-year periods.

While employers are responding to this movement toward stronger DEI, they are not yet making it a top priority. For instance, according to research by Jobvite (2018), while 60 per cent of recruiters agree that implicit bias is a real problem in the US workforce, only 15 per cent ranked 'increasing diversity at my company' as a top three priority for the ensuing 12 months. Perhaps more encouragingly, LinkedIn found in a 2019 survey that diversity was the top hiring priority, with 78 per cent of respondents saying it was 'extremely important'. LinkedIn is already adding tools to its platform to help recruiters improve their diversity ratios, and has begun to launch online education classes on subjects such as confronting bias, inclusive leadership and managing diversity.

Stages of the recruitment process

Let's walk through the stages of the recruitment process, and look at some ways to improve your chances for success at each stage.

Stage 1: Selecting the right recruiter

GET RECOMMENDATIONS

Speak to others who have a similar professional background to yours. Ask which recruiters they have used and – more specifically – which individual within the recruitment company they have worked with. You'll find a list later in this step of recruiters who are focused on the impact economy.

BE STRATEGIC ABOUT WHO REPRESENTS YOU

Work with one or two recruiters who best represent your interests in the sector in which you want to work. If you are working with multiple agencies it can become confusing knowing exactly what you have applied for and who exactly is representing you. Recruiters will be more motivated if you commit to working with them exclusively.

BEFORE YOU APPROACH A RECRUITER, CONSIDER SERIOUSLY WHETHER YOU WOULD ACCEPT A COUNTEROFFER IN YOUR CURRENT ROLE

If the answer is yes, think about negotiating your package with your employer prior to searching for a new job. If you turn down an offer that a recruiter has brokered to remain in your current position, you should expect that they may be frustrated. Often, they are working on a fee-on-success-only basis, so they may not be so helpful next time you need their assistance if they feel you've wasted their time. It is a two-way street, and you will get more out of them if you develop a firm and open relationship.

IF POSSIBLE, MEET FACE TO FACE WITH THE RECRUITERS YOU ARE WORKING WITH

This helps you to form a much closer relationship with your recruiter and shows a real commitment to the process. It also makes you more memorable, which means you may be top of mind when a promising role comes across their desk.

Stage 2: Building a strong relationship with your recruiter

GIVE THEM THE ESSENTIAL INFORMATION THE FIRST TIME YOU MEET WITH THEM AND BE TRANSPARENT

If they are good recruiters, they will want to gather a lot of information about you in order to best represent you to future employers. They will want to know details of the full benefits package you currently have or (more usefully) what you are seeking, realistic location requirements, reasons for being on the market, etc. You need to be willing to spend some time on the phone with them, as well as meeting face to face. Be open. Don't take offence if they ask you to amend your CV. They know best what their clients want, and their own personal success is based on making a successful match between you and an employer.

DON'T BE FORCED INTO INTERVIEWS OR DIRECTIONS THAT YOU DO NOT WISH TO INVESTIGATE

Set the goal posts at the start of the relationship, and make your requirements and desires clear. If you are working with a good recruiter, they may push back and advise you to look at other options. Remember that they are the experts and their advice is worth listening to so be flexible, but don't waste your time, the recruiter's time, or an employer's time by attending dead-end interviews. However, remember that some interviews are worth attending even if you are quite sure the opportunity is not right. A couple of hours invested in meeting an employer may come back to benefit you in the future.

Stage 3: Communicating with your recruiter

KEEP IN CONTACT WITH THE RECRUITER, BUT NOT TOO OFTEN

A fortnightly or monthly call is fine, but they are likely to be in touch with you should they have suggestions. Keep them informed of any circumstance changes (pay increases, change of location preferences, reduction in urgency of your job search, etc). But don't worry if they don't call you back. They are busy and it's not personal. They will take note of your ongoing interest though.

RETURN YOUR RECRUITERS' CALLS PROMPTLY

Recruiters want to work with responsive candidates, and if calls aren't returned it gives off bad signs. Conversely, if a recruiter doesn't return your calls over a period of time, consider whether they are the best suited to represent you.

BE OPEN WITH RECRUITERS WITH WHOM YOU ARE WORKING

If you are attending interviews with a number of organizations, let them know that is the case. The more open and honest you are about your employment search, the more likely the recruiter will be open with you regarding your suitability for specific roles and candid with their feedback.

Case Study   Rachel Gordon

With more than 15 years' experience advancing transformative healthcare and wellness solutions that improve lives across the pharma, fitness and consumer goods sectors, Rachel moved from freelance innovation consulting to work for Pepsi as its Director of Innovation. There she led a large, cross-functional transformation project that focused on developing new business models to move beyond drinks in plastic bottles. According to Rachel, it was 'the perfect culmination of my experience and interests'. Reflecting on her experience with recruiters, Rachel says, 'Working with recruiters has always been a bit of a mystery to me. But these key tips helped to demystify how they work, so that I could go into any conversation with the clarity and confidence I needed to help them help me.'

Recruiters specialized in the impact jobs market

Here are some recruitment firms that specialize in the impact jobs market. Make sure to research them thoroughly to find the best fit for you and your goals. You may also add to the list as you see roles posted. Even if the role isn't right for you at that time, make a note of who the agencies are and register your CV on their database or connect with the recruiter on LinkedIn.

US focus

- Acre Resources (health and safety focus);
- Blue Ridge Advisers;
- Isaacson, Miller;
- Janikin Rooke;
- Janssen & Associates (NGOs, foundations);
- Koya Leadership Partners;
- Leaderfit;
- Martha Montag Brown (NGOs, foundations);
- The Hanna Group (supply chain and logistics);
- Waldron (social impact);
- Weinreb Group (corporate sustainability).

UK and Europe focus

- Acre Resources;
- Allen & York;
- Amida Recruitment (built environment);
- Eden Brown (built environment);
- Environment Jobs UK;
- Evergreen Resources (environmental);

- Green Recruitment Company (energy, environment);
- Lancor (international development);
- Lewis Davey (cleantech);
- Mondo (communications);
- Oxford HR (international development);
- Peridot Partners (senior, NGO, education);
- Prospectus (NGO);
- The Sustainable Recruiter, The Netherlands.

Global focus

- Korn Ferry – Futurestep;
- Mission Talent (NGOs);
- Odgers Berndtson (NGOs);
- Perrett Laver;
- Russell Reynolds;
- Saxton Bampfylde.

Senior-level head hunters

- Egon Zehnder;
- Heidrick & Struggles.

KEY POINTS

In this step, we covered:

- what recruiters will do for you, and what they won't;
- how to approach recruiters in the purpose economy; and
- the stages of the recruitment process.

What's next?

Now that you've got a handle on how to navigate the recruitment process, we'll dive into the art of networking in the next step and put the finishing touches on the tools we need to get out there in the jobs market and find our dream role.

References and further reading

Holger, D (2019) [accessed 10 January 2020] The business case for diversity, *Wall Street Journal*, 26 October [Online] www.wsj.com/articles/the-business-case-for-more-diversity-11572091200 (archived at https://perma.cc/A7LT-6K9P)

Houde, S [accessed 15 September 2020] *Top 10 Sustainability Recruitment Agencies and How to Approach Them Part 2*, Walk of Life Coaching [Online] https://walkoflifecoaching.com/top-10-sustainability-recruitment-agencies-and-how-to-approach-them-2/ (archived at https://perma.cc/F4RQ-H2NE)

Jobvite (2018) [accessed 10 January 2020] *The Tipping Point: The next chapter in recruiting* [Online] www.jobvite.com/wp-content/uploads/2018/11/2018-Recruiter-Nation-Study.pdf (archived at https://perma.cc/9SKT-Y2CS)

LinkedIn Talent Solutions (2019) [accessed 10 January 2020] *Global Talent Trends 2019: The 4 ideas changing the way we work* [Online] business.linkedin.com/talent-solutions/recruiting-tips/global-talent-trends-2019?trk=bl-po# (archived at https://perma.cc/7XPX-X85J)

Pollak, J (2019) [accessed 10 January 2020] *Job Seekers Value Diversity When Looking for a Job, Cite Discrimination as Reason to Quit*, ZipRecruiter blog [Online] www.ziprecruiter.com/blog/job-seekers-value-diversity-when-looking-for-a-job/ (archived at https://perma.cc/L2V3-N58Y)

Networking sherpa

*How can I walk the talk of collaboration and
make new friends for a win–win?*

N ow that you've gotten a handle on the recruiting world and
how best to make it work for you, let's work on the dreaded
art of networking. This part is all about getting out there and
working your network of contacts on a regular basis. Success in
a job search or career change is all about who you know, and
growing that number of people can be key to finding the right
position and moving your CV to the top of the pile.

Why this step is important

According to GreenBiz (2018), fewer than a third of sustainability professionals landed their positions by applying through an
online job board. More than half heard about their job by word
of mouth or because the employer contacted them directly.
Networking is a key strategy for the jobseeker.

Leveraging your contacts is crucial to success, but building a strong network need not be a daunting process. This step will break it down so that you clearly understand how to build your own networking strategy, how to set realistic targets for reaching out, and how to write a powerful elevator pitch to wow your audience in person in just 30 seconds. It will highlight why networking isn't a dirty word or a chore; rather, it can fundamentally be about making new friends and expanding your circles of people who share your interests and passions.

Networking

Many people cringe at the thought of networking – it can feel uncomfortable and contrived – but it's up to you to get the word out and sell yourself. No one else is going to do it for you.

Right up front, let's establish that networks are all about mutual exchange. You can't just show up with a laundry list of needs, take what you find, and disappear. That doesn't work anywhere else in life, and it doesn't work in the jobs market. When you cultivate relationships, remember that they're a two-way street. Learn about the people you encounter, even if they can't give you a job tomorrow. Be interested in them. Care about their progression in their own careers, and elevate them whenever you have the opportunity to do so. Be genuine, authentic and compassionate in your interactions, and suddenly networking will no longer feel grubby; quite the opposite, it will feel like nurturing a community – because that's exactly what it is.

Why networking matters

There are two primary reasons why networking is important for an impact career.

Internal hiring and the hidden jobs market: Many open jobs are not even posted externally, so in order to increase your exposure to quality impact roles, you need to know someone on the inside. It's important to make personal contact with someone within the company before applying, as it's common for advertisements to be out of date or for the role to have been filled by an internal candidate who was slated for the role from the beginning. Even when the position is open, your chances increase substantially if someone walks your résumé over to the hiring manager. Don't forget about social media: leverage your connections on LinkedIn to get in front of people, as we discussed in Step 11.

TIP Convey your value

Companies often hire from within to fill sustainability jobs because they place a high value on the business and sector expertise that an insider brings. Highlight the sectors you know well to prove that you understand the competitors, stakeholders and product or service. This way it looks like you offer the same value as an internal candidate.

Collaboration and partnerships: The sustainability agenda is all about collaborating across sectors and departments to align stakeholders and build strategic partnerships for positive change. Think about networking as doing just that. Give yourself a shove and make it a goal to do one networking-related task daily. Those intimidating people hanging out around the water cooler at a conference are your future stakeholders and changemaker friends. More than likely, they are hesitant to network too, so jump in and collaborate. Ask what they are working on and how you can help. Ask them what their pain points are and who they're working with to move their agenda forward.

Building strategic partnerships in a sustainability role is the same as building your network to land a dream job. Think of all these people as friends, future colleagues and future partners in your mission. They are just people, after all.

Building a networking strategy

Jobseekers in the impact economy should devise a networking strategy with these four considerations in mind:

1 Who do you aspire to be? Follow people you admire on LinkedIn and Twitter. Find out how they got to where they are. Do a benchmarking study as an excuse to interview them and learn more about their career journey.
2 What companies do you think are really walking the talk? Follow them as well, and reach out to your existing contacts on LinkedIn to find out more about what is happening in terms of that company's talent agenda from the inside. How can you offer something now to help with their current pain points?
3 Map out why networking scares you and what you can do about it. Create a week-by-week plan to call three to four people a week for three months. By setting achievable and motivating goals for yourself and approaching the process step by step, you can avoid feeling overwhelmed. We'll talk about this a bit more later in this chapter.
4 Get your elevator pitch ready. Once you have practised it 20 times live, you'll feel confident in presenting it and will make a more lasting impression. Have both a written and verbal elevator pitch ready to go.

Once you start honing your networking techniques and see how fun it can be, you won't be able to stop. This skill will serve you long after you have landed the job. You will need it in any sustainability role aiming to bring others on board for innovative and lasting change.

Networking in the impact sector

The reason networking is even more important for sustainability work is that the agenda is still evolving and is uncharted territory compared with traditional commercial career tracks like finance, marketing, or operations. Many sustainability professionals accidentally fell into the role, or have only been in this space for less than five or ten years. The environmental agenda has gained so much traction over the last decade that companies are beginning to see the value in identifying risks and opportunities related to sustainability.

What this means, though, is that sustainability roles are not universally clearly defined, organizational charts are not standardized, and terminology is not consistent, so it's even harder to chart a job search. For all these reasons, networking is the number one way to get a job in sustainability.

People who have mastered networking follow three basic rules:

1 **Do it daily!** Each and every day, set one goal to do something 'networky'. Make a new contact, pick up the phone and call someone you read about, or ask a friend for a new lead. Sign up for conferences, events and LinkedIn, and branch out beyond your job description. Make connections across sectors, specialities, and levels of seniority. Doing one thing daily makes it less daunting, and you will gain momentum. It took me one year of writing blogs before I started hearing from new clients who actually read them. What we put into any endeavour is what we get out of it, and that holds doubly when we're networking for jobs. Remember the networking opportunity map we did in Step 2? Use that to keep track of your contacts and interactions, as well as new people you connect with along the way.

2 **Know your stuff.** Social media is an excellent platform for really getting to know the people and issues involved in your areas of interest, and it makes networking so much easier. Use LinkedIn, blogs, and Twitter to find out what people in your network are interested in and engage in the conversation. This is a great way to approach new people at conferences and business events, too: walking up to a complete stranger is

much easier if you know you can discuss a fantastic report you read on Twitter last week in their sector. The more informed we are about our sectors, the more interesting and valuable we will be to our expanding networks.

3 **Give to get.** Part of effective networking is getting to know people in the niche part of the sustainability sector you want to be in, people who hold your dream job, and learn their story. How did they get where they are? What did they learn along the way? What are their biggest challenges in their role now? Who do they use to recruit new talent? By the same token, it's important to give as well as take. How can you use your network to help your connections? Can you share ideas, articles and reports you've found useful? Can you help a contact with a challenge they're facing by introducing them to someone else you know? Perhaps refer others to jobs you have seen advertised? When we approach someone in our networks, it's important that we offer something in return.

Your network is worth its weight in gold when it comes to advancing your career in sustainability, so make sure you nurture it – daily!

Networking is like flirting

Walking up to a potential new contact at a conference, or cold calling someone on the phone, is often the most intimidating part of networking for jobseekers. It's hard to make the first move, and much easier to keep yourself out of a vulnerable situation. Networking is a lot like flirting, and it can be done artfully or awfully. To help take some of the agony out of the process, try following these steps.

ON THE ICE BREAKER

A lot of people struggle with how to make the first move. They wonder if they should ask to meet for coffee, request a phone call, or do something else altogether.

First, identify your target. It might be an industry leader you admire, or perhaps it's someone you know will be speaking at a conference you'll be attending. If you can talk to them in person, go for it! If not, reach out with email, InMail (LinkedIn's messaging system), or social media and try to set up a live conversation, preferably with video. Mention a mutual contact if you have one. Mention an article they may find useful for their work. Mention anything at all you may have in common after researching them as thoroughly as you can.

No matter how you reach out, come up with a compelling reason why you would like to talk to them. More than likely, if you seem interesting, and interested in them, they will find 10 minutes to talk to you.

Be confident. You'll never have the courage to start a conversation if you think that everyone in the room is smarter, more senior, or better dressed than you. Banish the imaginary hierarchy in your head and place yourself on an equal footing with everyone else, equally deserving of respect, equally worth talking to. Remember, you have a lot to offer, you are a good colleague to have, and you are valued and valuable. Good talent, not to mention friends, is hard to find, and your new contact will be looking to expand their network as well. That being said, the more informed you are about your niche, your sector, and the latest trends, the more interesting and valuable you will be to your expanding network.

ON MAKING THE MOST OF THE MEETING

What impresses you when someone approaches you? I have the best conversations with people who are knowledgeable and curious about their sector, but don't feel the need to have all the answers. They are comfortable with silence and don't let their nervousness turn into a babbling monologue. They are natural and not trying to sell me something, but rather find a way we might collaborate and share through our mutual passion for sustainability. They are comfortable with saying, 'that's a great question. Give me your card and I'll do some research and get back to you.' That's also an excuse to follow up!

This approach also demonstrates self-confidence, another important trait. Sometimes having the right attitude can supersede years of experience. You can work on this by building awareness of your top skills and unique selling points to help you speak naturally about yourself in both casual and more formal networking conversations. The more self-reflection you do ahead of time, the better off you'll be.

It's important to balance how much you talk and how much you listen. Having a little background knowledge on the company or individual will help the conversation flow, so do your research and prepare good questions in advance. Just like in dating; when in doubt, ask the other person to tell you about themselves. People love to talk about themselves, and this will leave them with a cosy feeling about you, even if you don't get a word in edgewise.

At the same time, it's a good idea to prepare a 30-second elevator pitch that sums up your unique selling points. A killer elevator pitch is concise, clear and confident, and ends with a clear question or request. Don't be shy to ask, and don't leave the person wondering what you want.

ON FOLLOWING UP IN STYLE

I can't stress enough how important it is to follow up in the days after a meeting or conversation. A short 'nice to meet you' email isn't just polite; it will remind key contacts of who you are, what you do, and what you have in common. Similarly, stay away from generic LinkedIn requests and always add a personal touch.

Remember that all relationships are a two-way street, so think about what you can offer as well as what you can receive. Nurture your network by sharing articles, insights and ideas. That way, when you need a personal recommendation or an internal referral, you're more likely to get a positive response.

Make sure to sustain your momentum by planning out your next steps after a big networking event or one-on-one meeting. Create a weekly plan to call three or four people a week for three months. Use LinkedIn as a tool to remind yourself to reach out to new contacts in four, eight and 12 weeks. Send them a birthday card? Or a work anniversary note? LinkedIn flags all these so nicely for you, so all you have to do is follow up.

HUMAN CONNECTION IN A REMOTE WORLD

As technological developments make it possible to conduct more and more of the human experience remotely, it's critical to foster genuine, human connection in our interpersonal relationships. This is just as true once you've got your dream job as it is when you're still trying to land it. We often hide behind texts and emails. Certainly, that can be efficient and expedient, but make the effort to do things in person when you can.

Conferences are a great place to see people in person, but of course that can get expensive. Consider using one of the apps that allow you to have video calls with people, no matter their location. I see almost all of my clients via Zoom video calls, for instance, and it allows me to build really strong relationships with them. It allows you to feel connected. Whatever approach you take, remember to cultivate the human connection in your interactions with people. It makes a huge difference.

Tips on networking at events

No matter how much of an extrovert you may be, you probably still feel a bit uncomfortable walking into a networking event. It's something about a room full of people already chatting to each other that is off-putting. Well there are some preparation tricks to help you overcome that imposter syndrome feeling and to improve your skills.

PREPARATION

Do your research on:

- the speakers and attendees;
- the latest information on attendees' organizations (latest press releases, etc);
- the subjects the speakers will cover (review the agenda in detail).

Be up to date on the topics. Read the news and research the focal areas of the conference/event.

Think of at least three conversation points or topics that fit the event and those attending.

Try to contact attendees you want to meet beforehand and ask for a few minutes with them at the event. Suggest a specific time and place based on the event agenda; if you don't, it's unlikely your meeting will happen.

AT THE EVENT

Arrive early. Get the lay of the land, look at the seating plan, and check out the exhibitor list (if relevant). If you're the sort of person who needs alone time periodically, see if you can find a quiet space to which you can escape every so often when things are in full swing. But be aware of not crawling away and using this as a place to hide and avoid putting yourself out there.

Be the introducer. Bring people together around common interests and issues. The more you do this for others, the more they will do it for you.

Be confident. (Fake it if you have to.) Approach people. Remember, most other people there are dealing with a room full of strangers too, just like you. And that first moment is the hardest, so just push through it.

Mingle. Make sure you keep moving every three to five minutes so you meet more people rather than getting too comfortable with the ones you are speaking to. Of course, if the conversation is really taking off and relevant, then stay with it, but if not, kindly slide away and on to the next person.

BREAKING IN

The worst part of networking is breaking the ice, finding that first thing to say to someone. But remember that most people in the room are also feeling uncomfortable and would be grateful if you did the heavy lifting of taking the first step. Everyone there is hoping to meet new contacts and to connect. The other people in the room aren't really that scary. Part of what holds us back in life is fear, but those who get ahead are the ones who push through that fear. A smile helps with that. Eye contact too. That said, pay attention to cultural norms. There are many countries in the world where shaking hands is not the standard. If you're going to be in a cultural context with which you're not especially familiar, take some time before you go to research appropriate greetings and comportment.

Being yourself is the most important. Come having prepared three things you want others to remember about you. If you don't prepare your messages, you may get stuck in small talk and not really connect. Plan your own introduction. Make it interesting. Have a good couple of lines about what you do. The 30-second elevator pitch can help here.

We all forget names, especially when we are a bit nervous. So when you first get introduced use a trick to remember their name and help them to remember yours. I say, 'Hi, I'm Shannon, like the river in Ireland, or... the airport.' Use their name three times in the conversation and then you won't forget it. This also helps you to use their name when introducing them to someone else who may enter your circle. When you introduce them, always include one fact that you learned about them to bridge the new person in.

CURIOUS TO CONNECT

The best way to connect is to ask others about themselves. Everyone loves to talk about themselves. Think of what you may want to know about them:

- 'So in what impact areas/SDGs are you trying to make a difference?'
- 'How did you get into sustainability?'
- 'What do you love about your work?'
- 'Where do you see your industry going in the next five years around combatting climate change?'
- 'What do you think the next big idea is going to be to save the planet?'
- 'What keeps you up at night?'

LISTENING AND BEING CURIOUS

Listening is about more than a head nod and reverting back to something about yourself. Try asking interested questions and then using active listening skills, summarizing what they said so they feel really heard. This will build a rapport and make them remember how you made them feel. Make them feel like they have all of your attention and try to resist letting your eyes wander the room looking for your next chat.

Think of ways you may be able to help the other person. Networking is a two-way street. Be curious about their challenges and ask what you can do to help them. Or offer to introduce them to someone you know at the event or via LinkedIn that could add value to their career or interest area.

Remember to pause and be intentional with your words before responding so that you are appropriate. Some issues may be fine to discuss with a stranger and others may be off limits.

STEPPING AWAY WITH GRACE

When you feel the conversation is dying down a bit, it is a good approach to lead on tying it up. You can politely say things like:

- 'So it looks like the next session is starting soon. It would be great to stay in touch and follow up in a few weeks/months to speak about X.'
- 'Are you going to the drinks event this evening? If so, I'll see you there and try to introduce you to X.'
- 'Thanks for the advice about the jobs market. Would you mind if I reached out in a week to follow up about your contact at company X?'

Before moving on to the next conversation, ask for their contact information and give them yours. You can do this in several ways. Business cards are the classic method, and they'll probably still be around for a few more years but they aren't great for the environment. You can also use your smart phones to transfer information, whether by sharing your contact cards with one another, or by using a business card replacement app. In 2020, an app called 'QR Me' was gaining a devoted following for its effectiveness and ease of use. It gives you a unique code you can bring up on your phone, and all the other person has to do is take a photo and it transmits your information directly into their contacts. You can also connect on the spot on LinkedIn.

Take a moment before the next session at the event to step aside and make a note of the person's name and what you discussed so you can remember details to mention in your follow-up.

FOLLOW UP

Though the event may be over, your work is not done. This is the time to follow up in a timely manner.

Update your contacts database and LinkedIn with your new contact within 48 hours.

Send a follow-up email to each person whose details you have within 24 hours referencing what you spoke about and any next steps.

If you had offered to help your new contact with something, follow up on this as well, as this earns you many points that may come in handy in the future.

Mark your calendar for a month or two in the future to send that contact a relevant article they may find interesting to show you are thinking of them and keep yourself front of mind. Again, this will make them remember how you made them feel.

WHAT NOT TO DO AT AN EVENT

Don't find the one person who looks familiar and stick with that person for the duration of the event. Stay away from your 'friends'.

Don't make the food table or bar your permanent home – although this is a great place to more comfortably break the ice.

Don't just wander the room saying hello to many different people without ever engaging in a full conversation.

Don't sit in the back of the room on your phone. Always sit down next to someone and introduce yourself and ask a question about them.

Tips on networking through LinkedIn

LinkedIn's premium membership allows you to use its InMail messaging platform to contact other users. Even if you stick with the basic membership, you can still purchase blocks of up to 10 InMails to use in a given month. Here are some tips for making the most of this approach to networking.

DEMONSTRATE VALUE

Like any other social media platform, people on LinkedIn get spammed. Your InMail should demonstrate what's in it for the recipient right out of the gate. Importantly, this value shouldn't be primarily about you or your job search, but rather about the person you're contacting and their business interests.

BE CLEAR ABOUT WHAT YOU WANT

Formulate a reasonable goal for your interaction – so, not that they offer you a job, but maybe a quick call or coffee – and state that goal explicitly. This is not the time or place to be coy or evasive. You may feel shy about your request, and hope that they'll take the bait and make the overture you're seeking. Resist this urge. Give the recipient the courtesy of clarity.

KEEP IT SHORT

InMails are a privileged means of contact, and they are also an interruption to the recipient's day. The most effective InMails are less than 100 words long, and demonstrate that you've done your research by being clear, specific and directed.

DON'T PITCH

LinkedIn is essentially a community, and as such, it's all about relationships. Its entire purpose is to create a network of professionals helping other professionals. Think of your InMails as conversation starters. They are your chance to see whether the recipient is open to more contact. Be human and conversant, while also being polite and respectful.

BASIC STRUCTURE

Your InMail should generally feature the following four ingredients, usually one sentence each:

- what you have in common: a mutual friend, school, client, or group you follow;
- where you've been: a few titbits about your career that make you interesting, insights you have about their business, etc;
- where you're going: what you're up to now and what you're aiming for;
- what you're asking of them: a call or meeting to discuss your career journey or learn about their sector, etc.

Here are two examples of an effective InMail:

Hello [name],

I found you through my contact/friend/colleague (pick one) [name]. Having worked for the European Parliament in Brussels in 2019, I am looking to move back after finishing my CSR degree at HEC in Geneva in August. I am a communications assistant with a three-year focus on conference/event planning and stakeholder engagement. I have lived/worked/studied in the UK, Belgium, Spain, Switzerland and Italy. Would you have 10 minutes for a phone call to give me insights into your fascinating career and international experience in CSR? I'd also love to share some of my ideas on education policy at the EU level.

All the best,

[your name]

Hello [name],

Company X is a phenomenal innovation company that I have been following for the past year. With 10+ years in healthcare at Fortune 100 company [name], I excel at the intersection of design, business and technology. I have partnered with [company names] on product innovation and can access high-profile companies through my [university name] MBA network. Company X needs me as its next Experience Strategist to scale its cutting-edge digital therapeutics products! I know you are a busy CEO, but would you have 10 minutes for a phone call so that I can share my proven market insights and business development ideas?

Many thanks for your time!

[your name]

PICK UP THE PHONE

To the extent possible, move to the phone to follow up on an InMail engagement. Punctuating your interaction with a human touch can do wonders for making you memorable, and can help to seal a new relationship.

The elevator pitch

Having a prepared, effective elevator pitch up your sleeve is essential if you want to make an impact in a job interview or at a networking event. It's an awkward moment and a missed opportunity to cross the path of an important client or work connection and find yourself dumbstruck by the 'So what do you do?' line.

Having an elevator pitch up your sleeve can help you out of those sticky situations and into the good graces of the person you're trying to impress. But first, here's an example of what **not** to do:

> '*I am a sustainability consultant who writes strategies and supports employee engagement for companies wanting to be more responsible. I can help management to identify their challenges, and sometimes design programmes to help turn the strategy into practice. I enjoy working with companies who care about the future.*'

While that statement may initially sound professional, if you really think about it, it doesn't tell us very much. It lacks specificity, outcomes, and a unique selling point, among other things.

Your pitch should communicate:

- what keywords you want the listener to remember about you;
- the value you bring in terms of impact;
- the unique benefits you bring to your area of work;
- how what you do is different from the competition – your unique selling points, names of companies you have worked with;

- your immediate objectives; and
- what you hope the person you're talking to can help you with.

So how do you do it? Get out that laptop and start writing! But beware, you don't have to have full sentences at the ready. It is better just to have some bullet points with keywords that you can easily remember when delivering it live. Here are 10 tips for a killer elevator pitch:

1 *Start with a hook.* This is the statement that makes the listener want to know more.

2 *Be concise.* Your pitch should be 30 to 60 seconds if said aloud, the equivalent of two to three floors in an elevator or around three sentences.

3 *Be clear.* Be clear about the problem you're solving and use simple and straightforward language, not in-depth technical details, so that even your granny would understand it.

4 *Be confident.* Effectively communicate the competitive advantage of your specific product or service. Be positive and proud of what you have done.

5 *Be enthusiastic.* Make your story come to life so that your listener wants to hear more. Make your enthusiasm contagious.

6 *Be visual.* Put yourself in a client or employer's shoes and paint a visual picture based on how you want them to feel if they work with you.

7 *Be skills focused.* Don't focus on roles or functions; instead, focus on your qualities or skills.

8 *Be targeted.* Know your audience well enough to weave in specifics that may interest them. Name drop companies you have worked with or for.

9 *Be goal oriented.* Once you identify your audience, you need to be clear what outcome you want from them. This is your call to action.

10 *End with a question.* To engage in the two-way conversation that makes for good networking, end with a question, such as, 'Tell me about yourself.'

Once you've done this, try it out. Start by recording a video of yourself presenting your pitch and play it back. Then see what feels good and what feels uncomfortable. It will take about 10 times delivering your pitch live and on the spot to really feel that it is natural and yours.

Trust your instincts and be yourself. Sleep on it, circle what works, edit, adjust and jiggle it around until you feel confident pulling it together. Remember, just like for job interviews, practice makes perfect: talk to a mirror or into your smart phone video recorder until you've got it just right.

Here's our previous example, reworked to follow the 10 tips above:

> *'I create strategies for small to medium-sized businesses that want to increase their competitive advantage through sustainability while also making profit. I have propelled the leadership forward on their sustainable business journey for Client 1, Client 2 and Client 3 (name them). I have a hands-on approach to implementing live projects, incentivizing employees to act and measuring impact with hard numbers. Getting clients clear on what is working and what isn't is key to how I add value. How does your organization balance making profits with having a positive impact on the planet and its people?'*

Elevator pitch examples

Consider the following elevator pitches. The 'before' examples represent really common formulations we hear, but they aren't especially effective. Pause after reading the 'before' examples and think for a minute about how they might be improved. Then have a look at the 'after' examples and see how they line up with your thoughts.

Before: 'I am a sustainability consultant who writes strategies and supports employee engagement for companies wanting to be more responsible. I can help management to identify their challenges and sometimes design programmes to help turn the strategy into practice. I enjoy working with companies who care about the future.'

After: 'I create strategies for small- to medium-sized businesses that want to increase their competitive advantage through sustainability while also making profit. I have propelled the leadership forward on their sustainable business journey for Client 1, Client 2 and Client 3 (name drop always!). I have a hands-on approach to implementing live projects, incentivizing employees to act and measuring impact with hard numbers. Getting clients clear on what is working and what isn't is key to how I add value.'

Before: 'I'm a social entrepreneur who helps companies be more sustainable.'

After: 'I consult with social enterprises. I only work with companies that have fewer than 20 people, and I only work with the founder. After building and selling my own social enterprise, [name], I'm confident of my niche, which is helping businesses make profit while having a social impact. Do you know any social entrepreneurs in London?'

Case Study   Adrianne Gilbride

Adrianne engaged her network to help her move from an environmentally focused project manager role into a wider sustainable business role in the outdoor apparel industry. Reflecting on how she used networking to her advantage, Adrianne says, 'It was refreshing to think about networking and my personal profile in new and creative ways. Developing my elevator pitch really gave me the confidence and motivation I needed to walk into any conversation and tackle my job search.'

KEY POINTS

In this step, we covered:

- how to network effectively both in your impact job search and as a professional in the purpose economy;
- how to network at events; and
- how to craft and deliver an elevator pitch for the impact sector.

What's next?

Now that you've developed your networking chops, we are closing in on the final step in this book. We need to talk about what to do once you land an interview for the role you've worked so hard to get!

References and further reading

Fine, D [accessed 15 September 2020] *Business Networking Skills/ Building Business Relationships*, debrafine.com [Online] https://www.debrafine.com/small-talk-expert/business-networking-skills-building-business-relationships/ (archived at https://perma.cc/ VLU7-VPP9)

GreenBiz Group (2018) [accessed 1 January 2020] *State of the Profession 2018* [Online] www.greenbiz.com/report/state-profession-2018-report (archived at https://perma.cc/AK7Q-7ZPW)

Houde, S (2013) [accessed 15 September 2020] *How Can I Sell Myself in a 30 Second Elevator Pitch*, GreenBiz.com (archived at https://perma.cc/ UM66-G5VD) [Online] https://www.greenbiz.com/article/how-can-i-sell-myself-30-second-elevator-pitch (archived at https://perma.cc/ 63V9-GDCB)

Houde, S (2017) [accessed 15 September 2020] *Dear Shannon: Breaking into the secret jobs market*, GreenBiz [Online] https://www.greenbiz.

com/article/dear-shannon-breaking-secret-jobs-market (archived at https://perma.cc/BX69-DRKZ)

Houde, S (2018) [accessed 15 September 2020] *How to Network Better than You Flirt*, NetImpact [Online] https://www.netimpact.org/blog/132086 (archived at https://perma.cc/B566-GD3E)

Houde, S [accessed 15 September 2020] *Ten Tips to Land Your Dream Job in a 30 Second Elevator Pitch*, Walk of Life Coaching [Online] https://walkoflifecoaching.com/ten-tips-dream-job-30-second-elevator-pitch/ (archived at https://perma.cc/F7LC-PC3Q)

Houde, S [accessed 15 September 2020] *3 Tips for Turning Networking into a Job*, Walk of Life Coaching [Online] https://walkoflifecoaching.com/3-tips-for-turning-networking-into-a-job/ (archived at https://perma.cc/6BDP-8FWA)

Now in person at the interview

How do I show them in person that I'm the one they want for the job?

Now that you've perfected the art of networking, we arrive at our final step! The interview is the last thing standing between you and the impact role you've worked so hard to get, so let's work on how you can nail it.

Why this step is important

After putting in the hard work to research and understand the role you want, fill in any skills gaps you might have had, and craft your personal brand story in a compelling way, now you have to prove your worth on the spot and show off your interpersonal skills. This can be a daunting part of the process, especially if you're not naturally quick on your feet. Fortunately, interviewing skills can be learned with the right effort and practice.

Remember, too, that this isn't just about the organization evaluating you. This is also another opportunity for you to get insight into the organization, and to make sure that it's really the right fit for you. This is where you test your theory that you've found your dream job.

How to nail the interview

The only way to succeed in this sometimes scary part of the job search is to prepare. Then, once you've thoroughly prepared, relax. That's a lot easier when you feel confident that you're ready. Here are tips for mastering every step of the interview process.

Preparation

DO YOUR HOMEWORK

Research the organization to death, even though you already did so when you were preparing your CV and cover letter. Find out even more about the organization, the person or people interviewing you, and the types of projects/clients they're working on/with.

Research the organization's competitors or peers, and read press releases or news articles related to the organization and its work. How has it differentiated itself from competitors or other actors in its space?

If you're interviewing at a publicly traded company, look up its most recent annual and quarterly reports and read them. If the organization publishes a sustainability or corporate responsibility report, read it.

Write down keywords related to the department and position for which you've applied. Be ready to weave what you've researched into your responses and questions during the interview. Make sure you evaluate and understand the organization's likely pain points, and be prepared to discuss how you will help to address those in your role.

DO YOUR SARS

SARs stands for situation/action/result. It is the framework for giving complete but concise answers to interview questions, also known as a competency-based interview. It helps to use this format in preparing for your interview so that your answers are clear in your head, and so you provide the necessary specifics in your answers.

Sit down and document possible questions the interviewer might ask about your experience and history related to every single requirement for the job. You should use the job-description rewrite you did in Step 6 to help you with this. Then, prepare your answers using the following format for each:

1 Briefly describe the *situation*.
2 Then describe the *action* that you took in the past or would take in the future.
3 Conclude by describing what the *result* of your action was or would be for the project, team, boss, company, or client.

Make sure to weave your five key skills words you developed in Step 7 throughout your answers.

PRACTISE

Ask a friend or family member to run through your SARs with you so that you can practise live. Even if it seems embarrassing, just take an hour to do this and it will pay off more than you know. It will help prevent you from stumbling over your answers during the interview itself.

PREPARE YOUR QUESTIONS

The interview is a two-way process. Come prepared with thoughtful questions for the interviewer as well. These might include:

- What will be my responsibilities?
- What will I be doing on my first day?
- Where will I fit into the overall organizational structure? Who will I report to?
- Where does my supervisor fit in the organizational structure?
- Who will report to me? What is their experience?
- Can you tell me a little about the team I'll be working with?
- What will you expect me to achieve in the first six months?
- What will be my goals and objectives in the first year?
- How will you evaluate performance in this role? What constitutes success?
- What is the organization's one- to five-year plan? Does it include plans for expansion or growth?
- What training do you provide?
- What are the opportunities for advancement in the organization?
- What are your/the organization's challenges?
- How would you describe the team and your management style?
- How does this organization develop and invest in its staff professionally (training, etc)?
- For consulting/advisory roles: What is the portfolio of clients/ projects I would be responsible for from day one?
- What skills do you see as most important for the challenges that come with this position?
- What will be some of the deciding factors in selecting a candidate for this role?
- When do you expect to select you're preferred candidate?
- What are the next steps in this process? (This is a key question to show you are 'closing', especially if you are interviewing for a business development or sales role. It's also important for you to know what to expect.)

The big day

BE PROFESSIONAL AND PREPARED

Reconfirm your interview the day before. Look up the map of where you're going and how to get there the night before.

BE FRESH AND ALERT BUT RELAXED

Avoid alcohol the night before, and give yourself time for a full night's sleep. Cut and clean your fingernails and polish your shoes. Don't drink too much caffeine before the interview. Always dress up, not down, if you don't know their dress code or how formal their work culture is.

Arrive 10 minutes early, and ask reception to direct you to the restroom so you can freshen up. Brush your teeth and wash your hands.

Bring a bottle of water with you in case they don't offer you any. Bring a pen, paper and a copy of your CV, along with notes on the company and the notes you've made for yourself. (Your notes can and should include the questions you've prepared to ask the interviewer, but make sure you're not reading your interview answers off a piece of paper!)

Smile when appropriate. Offer a solid and dry handshake, if culturally appropriate. Make eye contact with all interviewers, especially if there are more than one. These are all very important! Note that if you are interviewing internationally, this guidance may not be appropriate for all cultures, and you should research cultural norms ahead of time.

BE YOURSELF

The interviewer will want to see if you are someone they can work with. Just relax and be yourself!

> **TIP** In the impact sector, purpose is critical!
>
> If you're applying for a role of any kind in a purpose-driven organization, then no matter what that role is – whether it's in programmes and services, IT, accounting, or administration – it's imperative that you understand the organization's mission and how your role is expected to help meet it.

At the interview

Make sure to breathe before you answer. There is nothing to be gained from rushing through your responses and speaking too quickly. Stick to the SARs format you used in preparing your answers ahead of time, and don't forget to weave in your skills words.

Keep your answer to one minute, and pay attention to your audience to gauge their interest in and reaction to what you're saying. If you get the sense that you're not giving them the information they were looking for, don't hesitate to ask them to clarify their question.

After the interview

Follow up with a thank-you letter or email the next day. This is your chance to reiterate why they need you. It can also be an opportunity to supplement the answers you gave in the interview, in case you realize there was something important that you forgot to mention.

Possible interview questions

Guessing what the interviewer might ask is important so that you can practise, practise, practise. That said, there will surely be a few questions you won't have predicted. That's why it's important to do as much research as possible, and then to be relaxed in the interview and be thoughtful in your answers.

You should do your best to anticipate interview questions that are specific to the role and organization in question. Here are my favourite interview questions to get you generally ready:

1 How would you describe what we are looking for in this role?
2 What do you know about our organization, sector and competitive advantage/mission?
3 Why are you passionate about our organization's mission?
4 Where do you see sustainability (or corporate responsibility, etc) in the next five years?
5 You seem a bit over/underqualified for this role. What is your opinion?
6 Why should we hire you over the other qualified candidates we are interviewing?
7 What are your weaknesses?
8 What are your salary expectations?
9 Why did you leave your last job?
10 What is the riskiest thing you have ever done?
11 Where do you see yourself in five years?
12 What defines good communication?
13 What does it take to foster good teamwork?
14 How do you behave under pressure?
15 What would you do if you disagreed with someone, and how do you manage conflict?
16 How would you engage with and influence people to get their buy-in on a sustainability/impact initiative?

Here are some additional interview questions I've heard over the years:

1 Take me on a tour of your life.
2 How have you built key performance indicators around impact investing or ESG analysis? Please give an example.

3 How do you define yourself?

4 What am I not going to like about you after you've been here a few months?

5 What do you think you're not going to like about me?

6 If this situation were reversed and you were interviewing me because you had multiple job offers to choose from, what would you be asking me?

7 If you were in my position, and you were evaluating your candidacy for this role, where would you find shortcomings?

8 What percentage of your life do you control?

9 Can you force change to happen or will change happen to you?

KEY POINTS

In this step, we covered:

- how to prepare for and perform well in an interview; and

- possible interview questions you may field, particularly in the purpose economy.

What's next?

With that, we've got through all 14 steps of the journey to find your dream job in the purpose economy. Stick with me just a bit longer so we can tie everything together in the conclusion. Then you'll have what you need to get out there and find the good work you're so passionate about doing.

Conclusion

While we've reached the end of our book, this is just the beginning of your journey towards more fulfilling, purposeful work. In working through the 14 steps, you've armed yourself with the tools you need to get out there and land your dream job. You've developed an understanding of your aspirational impact job market, along with clarity and focus on what roles and sectors you want to target to make a difference to the planet and society. You've articulated your top skills and your career story, and have used those to maximize the effectiveness of your CV and cover letter. And you've enhanced your networking chops and crafted a compelling and effective LinkedIn profile.

More than that, hopefully you've realized that landing your dream job is a job in and of itself. It takes a lot of hard work and perseverance, some of which – like maintaining and nurturing your professional network – should ideally continue throughout your career. That's the beauty of following the steps: not only do they help you get a great job, they also make you better at that job.

There's no denying that the process is challenging. It's not easy confronting the reality that you're unhappy in your current situation, uncovering your biggest fears and deepest passions, and making the changes you need to reach your goals. But in doing so, you will find that you're constantly learning new things, and growing in directions that you never anticipated. The hard work is worth it, because it can lead you to a place where you're excited to wake up every day aligned to your purpose, instead of repeatedly hitting the snooze button or dreading the end of the weekend.

After all the specific work we've done throughout this book, the following takeaways are the most important:

- To land your dream job, you have to *believe in yourself*. Be confident and self-aware enough to be certain that you're the best person for the job, because if you're not convinced, they won't be.
- The impact economy is all about *relationships and people*, just like the sustainability agenda is. The way you influence and persuade people in an impact role is going to be very similar to how you do your job search for that role. Pass every conversation and written word through the lens of your audience. Practise empathy and hone your EQ. Get out of your own head and let yourself step into the shoes of your audience, whether the hiring manager or a networking lead. This is the transformational piece for my coaching clients, and when they truly take it on board, that's when they start to see positive momentum and feedback.
- Get comfortable with the *non-linear nature of the sustainability agenda*. It's evolving as fast as technology and social media, and there's no universal job path or career track for this. Accept and embrace that ambiguity, along with the initiative and creativity it will require of you in this job search process.
- Leverage the people who know you best and really let them help you. You need to *collaborate with someone else* on this

– don't do it in a bubble or in your own head. Recruit a career coach, friend, mentor, teacher, or family member to be your confidante in this process. Practise your elevator pitch with them, have them read your applications, and ask them to help you sound out your achievement statements before you put them to paper.

- Hope is not a strategy. To access and thrive in the purpose economy, it's not enough to sit back and look at the jobs boards online in the hopes it will all work out. It requires more from the jobseeker than a traditional job search. Don't underestimate the fact that it takes seven steps in this book to get to the point where you're ready to start crafting your written personal branding story. *The groundwork is key to your success.*

The opportunity in purpose

The good news for purpose-driven jobseekers is that the impact economy is growing. It must, if we are to address the serious challenges our world faces. As climate change risks loom ever larger, as population growth exerts increasing pressure on scarce natural resources, and as poverty and hunger persist across large swathes of the globe, the purpose jobs market requires an increasingly broad array of skills and experience from the people who work within it.

Purpose itself is reaching further than ever into the modern workplace, as a growing cohort of business leaders propose that companies of all stripes have an obligation to fulfil a broader social purpose than profit maximization. The Chief Executive Group posits that purpose and profit are even connected: 'When businesses are deliberate about prioritizing purpose beyond profit and are effective in how they serve a broad cross-section of societal constituencies – employees, suppliers, vendors and communities – results that favour the bottom line will be a logical outcome' (Ucuzoglu, 2020).

Career coaching

All of this means that it's a great time to go for it and make the leap into the impact economy. If you feel you could use more support, or if you want to get real-time guidance on the impact jobs market, you might want to consider seeking out a career coach who specializes in the purpose economy. A coach can help you dive deeper into the skills and resources you need to make your dream career a reality. They can help you refine your personal brand story, brush up on your interviewing skills, identify any skills gaps you may have, and much more.

Remember: life is too short to be stuck in the fog of a career without purpose or meaning. There's no time like the present to get out there and put in the hard work to do the good work that the planet and people need you to do.

Reference

Ucuzoglu, J (2020) [accessed 17 January 2020] Three megatrends could make or break your business this decade, *Chief Executive*, 17 January [Online] chiefexecutive.net/three-megatrends-could-make-or-break-your-business-this-decade/ (archived at https://perma.cc/CXN2-LQ5F)

INDEX

CPSIA information can be obtained
at www.ICGtesting.com
Printed in the USA
BVHW091010170221
600350BV00019B/363